Understanding Social Media

SAGE has been part of the global academic community since 1965, supporting high quality research and learning that transforms society and our understanding of individuals, groups and cultures. SAGE is the independent, innovative, natural home for authors, editors and societies who share our commitment and passion for the social sciences.

Find out more at: **www.sagepublications.com**

Understanding Social Media

Sam Hinton and Larissa Hjorth

Los Angeles | London | New Delhi
Singapore | Washington DC

Los Angeles | London | New Delhi
Singapore | Washington DC

SAGE Publications Ltd
1 Oliver's Yard
55 City Road
London EC1Y 1SP

SAGE Publications Inc.
2455 Teller Road
Thousand Oaks, California 91320

SAGE Publications India Pvt Ltd
B 1/I 1 Mohan Cooperative Industrial Area
Mathura Road
New Delhi 110 044

SAGE Publications Asia-Pacific Pte Ltd
3 Church Street
#10-04 Samsung Hub
Singapore 049483

Editor: Mila Steele
Assistant editor: James Piper
Production editor: Imogen Roome
Copyeditor: Solveig Gardner Servian
Indexer: Indexing Specialists Ltd
Marketing manager: Michael Ainsley
Cover design: Naomi Robinson
Typeset by: C&M Digitals (P) Ltd, Chennai, India
Printed in India at Replika Press Pvt Ltd

Figure 5.3: Artist: Cao Fei
Medium: Second Life
Courtesy of *RMB City* © 2012
RMB City Project is developed by Cao Fei (SL: China
Tracy) and Vitamin
Creative Space
Facilitator: Uli Sigg (SL: UliSigg Cisse)
Public Presenter: Serpentine Gallery (London)

Library of Congress Control Number: 2012951705

British Library Cataloguing in Publication data

A catalogue record for this book is available from
the British Library

ISBN 978-1-4462-0120-6
ISBN 978-1-4462-0121-3

Contents

Acknowledgements

Firstly, the authors would like to thank series editors Jen Webb and Tony Shirato and Sage's Mila Steele for their help in developing this publication.

Secondly, we would like to thank the wonderful community of researchers who are exploring social media for all your insights, inspiration and thoughtful provocations. We would also like to acknowledge the support of the University of Canberra and RMIT University, Melbourne.

Sam would like to thank his family, friends and colleagues in media, arts and production, who gave him both the time and space to bring this book together, and to his co-author, Larissa Hjorth, whose energy and intelligence pushed this book through from draft to conclusion. Sam would like to dedicate this book to his family: Nicole, Catherine and Sarah – you three continue to humble me.

Larissa would like to thank the Australia Research Council for a discovery grant (DP0986998) that allowed her the time to conduct empirical research for this book. She would also like to thank family and friends and dedicates this book to her son, Jesper, and brother, Greg.

1 Introduction to social media

It's 9 p.m. and in the busy streets of Shanghai, a Chinese teenager takes a picture via her iPhone and loads it up to her social network site (SNS), Renren. Meanwhile, a high school boy in Manila logs on to his Facebook page via his personal PC to say hello to his aunty who has just woken up in LA. Elsewhere, two university friends in Seoul stay up late to play a social media game in their local *PC bang* (PC internet room), while another university student in Beijing logs on to FarmVille to play with their parents in a far away village. In London, two high school students sit together editing and commenting on their Facebook pictures in a local café. At the same time, two old friends meet up face-to-face in New York for breakfast, thanks to Facebook Places.

These fleeting moments of connection take place through flashes of light, across deep-sea cables and microwave pulses that bounce invisibly between orbiting satellites. If we could see these connections plotted around the globe, the world would be illuminated like an exquisite decoration, shimmering with the mediated social interactions of many of its nearly seven billion inhabitants. Today, social media in its many forms accounts for a great deal of this mediated activity. Social media bleeds across platforms (desktop computers, mobile phones, tablets and on modern network-capable televisions), across social and media contexts, and creates various forms of presence. As smartphones continue to move into mainstream everyday life in many urban settings globally, the demographics of social media are also changing. Once upon a time, SNSs were just for the young (boyd and Ellison 2007), but today young and old can be seen using SNSs in everyday life.

As SNSs evolve, the term 'social media' is also developing to encompass the growing and often unwieldy sphere of contemporary online media practice. For Melissa Gregg, social media accompanies a movement towards 'presence bleed', 'where boundaries between personal and professional identities no longer apply' (2011: 2). Underlying this concept is an array of questions about the changing nature of what is public and what is private, and where work ends and life begins, as social media infiltrates every facet of everyday life.

For danah boyd, SNSs are a genre of what she calls 'networked publics' (2011), that is, public groupings that are structured by the logic and reality of computer networks. For Mark Andrejevic, the 'networked sociabilities' of SNSs are ordered by a 'separation of the user from the means of socialising, thus permitting "storable and sortable" collections of social data' (Andrejevic 2011: 311). In other words, the social activities of the user can be easily adapted by social media companies into 'user profiles' that are then sold to advertisers. This phenomenon has led media activist and theorist Geert Lovink to argue for alternative models of social media beyond the stronghold of mainstream companies like Facebook and Google (2012).

Understanding Social Media attempts to engage with some of these complex debates about the definitions of social media. We reflect upon the differences between SNSs and social media and how the rise in devices such as smartphones and locative media services such as Facebook Places, Google Maps, and Foursquare are changing the fabric of social media. We acknowledge that social media is currently transforming definitions of both 'social' and 'media'.

Social media impacts on the way in which we think, experience and practise 'online media'. It is no longer merely a form of teen socialising – it has become an integral part of everyday life. In turn, this influences how we reflect and engage with friends, family, colleagues and politics. Social media further amplifies the changes in the media landscape and as it does, it provides new avenues for dissemination and engagement. For some critics, social media is part of the rise of participatory culture which empowers users (Jenkins 2006) to produce their own content, to become 'produsers' (Bruns 2005). For others, social media is part of broader 'structural affordances of a capitalist economy' (Andrejevic 2011: 312) in which users' free labour is exploited for the benefit of corporations (Kücklich 2005; Andrejevic 2011; Lovink 2012). For still others, the relationship between production and consumption has now altered and should not be understood in the same way that sociologists understood production in an industrial context (Banks and Humphreys 2008). The widely varying ideas, criticisms and exhortations about social media reflect the complex social processes that it engages with.

In order to address these issues, and provide a framework for understanding the many different concepts and theories that inform the debates surrounding social media, we deal with four recurrent themes throughout this book. These themes are: empowerment/control, online/offline, the role of the local/cultural (especially in non-Anglophonic contexts) and the 'intimacy turn'. The first two themes present as dichotomies. However, rather than seeing them as an 'either/or' relationship, we suggest that the reality is somewhere in the middle, and their apparent oppositions provide us with two ways in which we can critically examine social media. So, social media is neither entirely empowering nor entirely controlling. In fact, it is often both.

Likewise, it is important to acknowledge that social media contains offline modes of engagement: it is never entirely just an online phenomenon. Given that social intimacy has always been mediated (Hjorth 2005), the online/offline tension suggests new entanglements for social interaction, notions of presence and its impact upon public and private spaces. The relationships that people have online are always shaping, and shaped by, the offline. This may be as obvious as the recognition that our online friends are frequently people we know from home or work. Or it may be as subtle as understanding that how we behave online, who we choose to make friends with online, and how we use our online time are all influenced by the reality of our offline lives.

The final two themes – non-Anglophonic contexts and the intimacy turn – respectively focus our attention upon the global and local nature of social media. In this book, we want to emphasise the truly global nature of social media by mixing Anglophonic and non-Anglophonic perspectives. We seek to bring balance and emphasise the socio-cultural nature of social media in light of the dominance of Anglophonic approaches (Goggin and McLelland 2009). This not only serves to highlight how different cultural perspectives change the meaning of certain concepts (like privacy, for example), but also serves as a foil to help us better understand how our own cultural practices involve assumptions and tacit knowledge. The local continues to play a key role in the uneven global evolution of social media across a variety of platforms, modes of presence, contexts and media.

Even intimacy operates upon micro (individual), meso (social) and macro (cultural) levels as a glue for social relationships. When we refer to the 'intimacy turn', we are drawing attention to the way in which the concept of intimacy can be used to understand some of the erosions between public and private spaces, and between work and leisure in contemporary societies (Berlant 1998). To put it another way, social media affords certain kinds of social performance that involve making intimacy more public. For example, when a Facebook user takes and uploads self-portraits, they may well only intend these to be viewed by an audience of close friends even though they have their privacy settings set to public. However, with Facebook owning the copyright of the pictures, which are available to be seen by anyone with a Facebook account, how the pictures would be recontextualised and further consumed is complex and little understood. Alternatively, a user might have their personal photo albums set to be viewable only by family and friends, and so the viewing activity becomes a semi-public performance.

Such constructions of contemporary online identities reminds us of sociologist Erving Goffman's work on impression management, especially his use of the analogy of the theatre stage (with its frontstage and backstage spaces) in *The Presentation of Self in Everyday Life* (1959). With the 'context collapse' of social media (boyd 2011) it is not uncommon to see users having more than one Twitter and Facebook account for different 'public' and 'private' contexts. Friendship and intimacy can be both amplified and commodified through social media.

Through these four themes, *Understanding Social Media* explores the fabric of social media today. By no means exhaustive, this book seeks to provide case studies that allow for reflection upon the changing nature of social media. It is structured into six main chapters, an introductory chapter and a concluding chapter. Each chapter deals with a different subject and its relationship with social media, and acts as a vehicle to explore the four themes that run through the book.

Chapter 2 explores the rise of Web 2.0 as a way of contextualising the ideological environment in which social media operates. Rather than presenting Web 2.0 as a revolution in the way the web 'works', as some have, we take a more critical stance. We examine the way in which Web 2.0 functions as an ideology that declares the corporate world's growing understanding that the internet is not only mass, but also social, media. We then look at both the empowering and the controlling elements that go hand in hand with Web 2.0.

Chapter 3 engages with the undisputed icons of social media, social network sites or SNSs. Here we contextualise SNSs within a tradition of internet studies which has been conducting research and enquiry into the nature of online communities for more than two decades. Without attempting to deny their novelty, we emphasise that SNSs represent a continuity with earlier ways of thinking about the social aspects of the internet. In this chapter, we look at how in the field of internet studies, early notions of the internet as a series of virtual communities have yielded to more recent ideas of SNS practices and discourses as involving 'networked publics' and 'intimate publics'. We also engage with a number of other research approaches to SNSs in order to define the field.

With a more thorough understanding of SNSs and some of the ways they have been theorised in place, Chapter 4 returns to the themes of control and empowerment we introduced in Chapter 2, and applies them to practical examples of social media in action. In this chapter we look at how internet participation can yield user created content (UCC) and how it has allowed the figure of the 'produser' (Bruns 2005) to emerge. We describe this as being a potentially empowering outcome of social media, and examine how produsage is present in online activism and citizen journalism. We then consider how the intimate turn has challenged traditional models for journalism (Goggin 2011) and how participative media is destabilising the established power structures of governments and what Dan Gillmor refers to as 'Big Media'.

Just as participative media is challenging the status quo in politics and journalism, it is also challenging the established structures in other spheres of life. In Chapter 5 we examine cultural production and focus on how social media is precipitating and reflecting changes in the arts as a specific site of cultural production. We look at how cultural institutions such as galleries and museums are responding to new challenges by embracing Web 2.0 inspired notions of social media and how this is displacing their traditional roles as arbiters of taste. We examine how artists are responding to social media, and how the emergence of art-themed SNSs like deviantArt are challenging conceptions of art production and consumption as well as distinctions between the amateur and the professional artist. Finally, we examine the cultural complication of what Jean Burgess has termed 'vernacular creativity' (2007).

In Chapter 6 we look at games, a realm which has always been associated with the social. Here we look at how social media and games intersect in the form of SNS games – games that are played within SNSs and take advantage of features such as friends' lists to add a social dimension to their practice. While social games offer new types of places to play and socialise, they also involve two forms of labour. First, time spent playing online games raises money for the SNSs and game companies through advertising and in-game purchases. Second, since social games are a way to socialise, playing games is also a way to maintain contacts and thus provide the means to maintain social capital. In this chapter, we explore the role that social games play in maintaining inter-generational ties in China as a case study. Specifically, we examine how social games act as a way for youth who have moved away from home for work or study to maintain relationships with their families.

In Chapter 7 we reflect upon the convergence between social, locative and mobile media, and upon the uneven journey of the mobile phone's role in this. In particular we look at how location-based services (LBS), such as Google Maps and Facebook Places, have converged with mobile and social media through the smartphone. We look at how mobility has become about more than the ability to take your social media with you as the popularity of such devices has grown. Specifically, there are two results: the expansion of cartographies enabled by LBS devices and mobile apps; and the development of location-based social apps that blend social relationships with geography.

These changes reflect broader shifts in the relationships between identity, place and community and raise important issues about privacy, but also how we narrate and attach meaning to place. This chapter also considers the changing role camera phones play in our understandings and visualisations of place, especially as they become entangled in locative media practices.

We end with a brief conclusion that summarises the main themes of the book. While we have written the chapters in this book to flow from one chapter to the next, the book can also be read randomly one chapter at a time. When concepts come up in each chapter that have been covered elsewhere, we refer the reader back to the relevant chapter. The major themes we cover in the book – empowerment and control, online and offline, non-Anglophonic contexts and intimacy – are woven into and across the chapters. You are encouraged to cherry-pick the pieces in the book that interest you if that method of reading suits you best.

2 What is Web 2.0?

Markets are conversations (Levine et al. 2000)

Focus on the user and all else will follow (Google).

> Once the internet changed the world; now the world is changing the internet. Its mainstreaming is well and truly over, and the forgettable Web 2.0 saga has run its course. Now that society has overruled their freewheeling ethic, the notion of the internet as an exceptional, unregulated sphere evaporates. The moment of decision bears upon us: which side are you on? (Lovink 2012: 1)

As Lovink's quote above suggests, the internet is coming of age. With more than a decade of use in many parts of the world, the internet is embedded in the everyday. But along with its uneven development across the globe come issues concerning power and locality. There are many internets across the world, accessed and used in a variety of ways. In this chapter we engage with one of the major themes that underlie the emergence of social media: the tension between control and freedom and between exploitation and empowerment. We look at how business interests have attempted to commercialise the internet and how, over the course of a decade, they have shifted their strategies in order to align with how people are actually using the internet. This transition to user-focused business models is represented in the term 'Web 2.0'.

To begin this chapter, we indulge in a brief discussion of the web, highlighting the key technical features and its relationship with the development of the internet. When we think of the internet we must acknowledge that it encompasses multiple definitions and experiences. Rather than 'one' internet, there are multiple, intersecting imaginings and understandings of the internet that are informed by the user's background and experiences. The internet is not a parallel universe (as was suggested by early writings on cyberspace) but rather has always been a part of everyday life. Today, with the popularity of 'always on' mobile media allowing users to perpetually surf across social and locative media apps, the internet has become an embedded part of mundane social life.

For Lovink, the rise of Web 2.0 heralded a new definition of the term 'social' that no longer evokes the possibility for democratic empowerment and change as it did in the nineteenth or twentieth centuries. Instead, the 'social' has been tamed (2012: 6). As Lovink notes, '[p]latforms come and go, but the trend is clear: the networks without cause are time eaters, and we're only being sucked deeper into the social cave without knowing what to look for' (2012: 6). Representing internet culture as being 'caught between self-referentiality and institutional arrangements' (2012: 2), Lovink observes that:

> It is no longer sufficient to complain about network society's dysfunctionalities in terms of usability, access, privacy, or copyright infringements. Instead, we need to investigate the slippery nexus between the internet's reinforcement of existing power structures, and parallel – and increasingly interpenetrating – worlds where control is diffused. (2012: 2)

In order to understand the current tensions around the relationship between internet cultures and the social, this chapter investigates the often-confusing notion of Web 2.0 so that some clarity can be brought into our understanding of social media. Unpacking social media necessitates us tracing how internet cultures have shaped, and been shaped by, the social. In this book we try to expand upon the often Anglophonic or Eurocentric assumptions residing behind notions of the social, cultural and technological (Goggin and McLelland 2009). We are also trying to avoid repeating the historical narratives that describe the development of the internet and the web because our goal here is to provide a broad context. Internet and web history has been done well elsewhere, and we strongly encourage you to read one of the recommended texts on internet history if you have not already done so.

Once we establish a shared understanding of the web, we will then go on to examine how business, through the problematic term 'Web 2.0', has come to understand the internet as a place where people, and organisations, engage with each other in a 'conversation'. This realisation, which is a central philosophy of Web 2.0, represents an important shift away from mass media conceptualisations of audiences and a re-imagining of the internet user. The last part of this chapter examines Web 2.0 and social media more critically, engaging with the contradictions between freedom, control and empowerment that, as Wendy Chun (2006) has so eloquently explained, coexist in the reality of contemporary networked media.

BACKGROUND: WHAT IS THE WEB?

While the internet was developed from the late 1960s, it was not until the early 1990s that the web evolved into what we understand as the 'online' today. Prior to the advancement of the web, the internet was made up of a series of computers, connected to each other through numerous diverse methods but sharing a common basic data transfer protocol called TCP/IP. Each of the computers connected to each other via the internet were able to share data with each other, and as the internet developed, the ability to locate (or 'discover') resources became an increasingly large problem. The web provided an interface that allowed people to discover and access internet resources quickly and easily.

The TCP/IP protocol describes how data on one computer can be transferred to another computer across a vast network made up of anything from physical copper wires to wireless satellite connections. TCP/IP does not decipher the data, it just deals with lumps of zeros and ones – called packets – and makes sure each packet is delivered to the correct computer in the right order without any loss of data. On top of this protocol sit 'application protocols', which are concerned with making sense of data. Email is one such application protocol. The email protocols describe how an email can be turned into small chunks of information, sent over the TCP/IP protocol to another computer and then reassembled as an email at the other end. The web constitutes just one of these application protocols – a protocol called HTTP, or hypertext transfer protocol – but because the web is the main way in which we interact with the internet on a daily basis, people often conflate the terms 'internet' and 'web'. In day-to-day circumstances that is probably fine, but when we think about these things critically it is important to be precise.

For most people, the primary experience with the internet is through the web browser – of which there are many different brands such as Firefox, Internet Explorer, Safari and Google Chrome. While each of these browsers has slightly different features, they all use the same HTTP application protocol for sharing information across the internet, and they are all designed to assemble text, images, video and interactive components together into one coherent interface. It is this interface – which we call the web page – that constitutes our experience of the web. Because the browser is so good at assembling different kinds of media and presenting them in a single unified interface, the web browser becomes most people's entire interface with the internet.

The other important piece of software on the internet that makes the web possible is the web server. The server is a computer program that is constantly running on a computer that is always connected the internet. The software waits until someone contacts it, and then responds to this contact by sending data – mostly text and images, but often also things like video or perhaps interactive content like games. When you type in a website address (called a URL or Uniform/Universal Resource Locator) you are typing in the name of a computer on the internet (called a 'host') and also specifying what resource you want to retrieve from that host. Clicking on a hyperlink does the same thing – the URL is contained in the hyperlink. The server is a vital piece of software, and although it can be installed and run on any computer that is connected to the internet, most organisations purchase dedicated computers which are optimised to run server software. A busy website may in fact require several servers to share the load, although through various techniques these often appear as only one site as far as the person accessing the website is concerned.

It is essential to understand that communication between a browser and web server is always two-way – the browser sends information about what it wants to access, and the server responds with the information, or an error message if it doesn't have the requested information. This is different from a technology like radio or television where the receiver never sends information, only receives it. This two-way communication is fundamental to the way the web works, and, as we will see below, this has a number of important implications for the way that people can, and do, use the web. In particular, this two-way process means practices such as participation and collaboration become increasingly possible and relevant to the fabric of the internet.

We could go into a discussion of the people and events that surrounded the development of the web in the early 1990s, but there are other references that do a great job of this (such as Bell and Kennedy's *The Cybercultures Reader*). An important factor here is the idea of hypertext – that is, the methods of making text interactive – which was invented by Ted Nelson in 1963. By the 1970s and 1980s, hypertext was playing a pivotal role in computer applications and design of the web.

For Tim Berners-Lee – the inventor of the World Wide Web – hypertext was crucial in the designing of the web as part of a networked environment. Berners-Lee's contribution was to use hypertext to link texts that could be located on any computer on the internet. This meant that texts could be connected to other texts, forming a complex series of relationships that Berners-Lee visualised as a web-like structure, hence the name 'web'. Not only did this make accessing resources much easier, it also made discovering resources much easier. Before long people were setting up web servers that presented lists of links to other web pages which contained information they found useful.

The other important thing that the web provided was a single piece of software for handling different kinds of media. Apart from text and hypertext, the web can also allow computers on the internet to share images, audio, video and other forms of media. When these are mixed together, the result is a multimedia interface – a single view that can incorporate elements of many different media. Almost every web page you access contains a variety of media elements.

The web quickly became the quintessential 'killer app' – a phrase that denotes a software application that is so successful that it sells the platform that it runs on. Early killer apps sold computer platforms, and the web, if seen in a similar light, has sold the internet, at least in a metaphorical sense. The growth in internet use is closely correlated to the development of the web and, although we should always be careful not to confuse correlation with causation, it seems quite clear here that the web's ability to bring together multiple digital media sources through a single easy-to-use interface was a significant innovation in the development of the internet.

COMMERCIALISING THE WEB

In this section we explore the ways in which businesses have tried to commercialise the web, and how an initial understanding of the web as a kind of television station with many channels has given way to a more nuanced definition. An important part of this shift has been the realisation that media was no longer delivered in a sealed package to audiences but that audiences played a participatory role in its creation (Jenkins 2006). The commercialisation of the web is marked by this change in attitude, which is described in business literature as the emergence of Web 2.0. For critics such as Lovink (2012), this commercialisation not only profits from the labour and creativity of internet users, but also simplifies the complex history and definition of the 'social' into little more than a prefix for Web 2.0 practice (i.e. 'social media').

We will come back to analyse the term 'Web 2.0' a little later in this section. For now, we use Web 2.0 as a placeholder within a discussion about the commercialisation of the web. Because Web 2.0 is a term that is fundamentally derived from the logic of capitalism, marketing and commercialisation, it seems reasonable that we should mobilise it in this critical examination. Thus, in this section, we will arbitrarily break the discussion of the commercialisation of the web into two segments, separated by the emergence of the term Web 2.0. In deference to this term, we will start with the period preceding it, a time that logically (from a software development perspective, anyhow), is defined by the term 'Web 1.0'.

WEB 1.0

Web 1.0 is a phantom term, constructed after the event. People did not speak of Web 1.0 until after the concept of Web 2.0 had been defined. In this respect Web 1.0 is an arbitrary historicisation, not much different from the way historians used to break history into the time before the birth of Jesus Christ (BC), and after (AD). Just as nobody walked around Europe 2,500 years ago talking about how nice it was to be living in 500BC, nobody talked about Web 1.0 until the term Web 2.0 emerged. The tag '2.0' evokes the idea of software versioning and its associated marketing,[1] and so suggests that Web 1.0 was less evolved, less sophisticated and less refined.

In the introduction to this chapter we suggested that the web was a significant factor in the rapid development of the internet. In a field that is quite liberally scattered with hyperbole and invective, the one fact that is probably fair to say is that the growth of the internet has been nothing short of remarkable. With so many people going online so quickly, it was only a matter of time before companies started to realise the potential of this medium. Where there are people, there are markets, and the internet, which is by design a two-way digital medium, had the potential to offer up something that mass media broadcast technologies could not: a source of highly detailed information about audiences.

Inevitably, initial attempts by large companies to control this digital environment were based upon their experience with traditional media. Television used content to aggregate audiences with similar interests: a science-fiction show attracted a certain demographic, soap operas another, and so on. Consequently, an apparently reasonable strategy in the online space was to accumulate attention, in a similar way, and then to sell products and services to a captive audience. Attracting attention in the online environment proved to be relatively easy, but turning that attention into money was problematic.

Commercialisation of the web has not been the straightforward process that many early internet entrepreneurs felt it might be. Roger Clarke (1999) has suggested that one of the key problems for those looking to make money from the internet in the early days was a simple unwillingness of internet users to pay for online services. Straightforward subscription models were only marginally successful and many initial attempts to set up internet pay sites were undermined by other sites that gave away information in a rush to build large user-bases.

Web 1.0 emerged out of a desire to make money from internet users, or to 'monetise' them (to use the rather ugly word that is widespread in marketing and business circles). It also built on pre-internet dreams which involved computer services of some kind that would be delivered to the home: at this time, the idea of the domestic computer service has been an ongoing theme in the media, information technology and telecommunications sectors for almost four decades (Haddon 1999). Attempts by businesses to establish information networks in people's homes before the internet emerged as a viable domestic networking technology – such as Videotex – were largely unsuccessful and generally very expensive mistakes for the companies that backed them.

Nevertheless, undeterred by past experience, and spurred on by the phenomenal growth rate of the internet subscription base, entrepreneurs courted the internet as a commercial domestic network as soon as user numbers began growing in the mid-1990s. Despite initial enthusiasm, the commercialisation of internet users (as distinct from commercialisation of internet access, which was very successful for major ISPs and telecommunications companies) proved to be highly elusive.

Wired magazine claims that it was the first organisation to launch banner ads on its website Hotwired in October 1994 (Clarke 1999). Other companies followed this trend, and there soon began a rapid appearance of advertising banners on search engines and other websites. This was a substantial imposition on the slow, low-bandwidth connections of the time. Although this kind of advertising has since proven one of the more effective ways for websites to make money, these initial attempts were less than successful. As Clarke pointed out:

> The investments made in electronic marketing proved to be anything but 'patient money', however. Little over 12 months after Hotwired's launch, another *Wired* author wrote of 'The Great Web Wipeout', with such heralded new businesses as The Spot, *The New York Times* site, and Hotwired already licking their wounds. (Clarke 1999)

This initial failure was blamed on technological and economic factors. The argument was that the web was simply not (yet) capable of maintaining internet commerce, the network was not technically sophisticated enough and slowed things down too much, and as soon as sites and services became popular they crumpled under the weight of user attention. There was a certain amount of truth to this, although there was an underlying lack of interest in actually attempting to understand how people were using the internet, and how this affected business models that were still treating internet users like TV audiences.

As an extension of success enjoyed by some of the non-internet online services that had emerged in the 1980s (Compuserve and AOL, for example), some internet entrepreneurs attempted to create internet services that provided the same kind of isolated walled-off space, but on the internet rather than on a proprietary online system. Microsoft even attempted to establish the Microsoft Network (MSN) as its own proprietary network quite apart from (and perhaps imagined to compete with) the internet. The idea was to get users to sign up for an online service that integrated directly into Microsoft's desktop environment – Microsoft's plan here was to use their market dominance in operating systems to establish a new online service. Generally speaking, such 'gated' areas of the internet also failed to appeal to users, and were not successful in generating revenue. Why voluntarily stay behind a walled-off zone that you have to pay subscription fees to live within when there's a free garden of earthly delights just a modem's dial away?

The failure of MSN was a particularly significant experience for Microsoft who, until this time, had gone from strength to strength with almost every new product or idea achieving immense commercial success. Within months of launching MSN, Microsoft relegated the service to a content-aggregation node of the internet, making a hasty about-face. A previously unknown software company – Netscape – became a multi-million dollar business virtually overnight by giving its web browser software to users and selling web server software to companies.[2] One of the young engineers who helped establish the company found himself on the cover of *Time* magazine, declared one of a new breed of 'instantaires' (Collins, 1996).

While academics had been developing more sophisticated understandings of internet users through the 1990s – as we will discuss in the next section – John Hagel's 1997 *Net Gain* attempted to explain how online communities could be considered an important commercial resource. According to Hagel, the aggregation of internet communities around certain areas of interest provided an opportunity for so-called 'info-mediaries' to deliver audiences to advertisers and marketers. This concept was engaged with literally by some businesses, who then constructed web portals – sites that aim to aggregate users around centralised content – in an attempt to concentrate user attention.

Because of their importance for internet resource discovery, search engines formed some of the earliest portals. America Online (AOL), and certain other companies who provided dial-in access, sought to aggregate users by channelling them into their sites as the user connected to the internet. But, aggregation of users was only part of the problem. The more difficult goal was to make money from those users in some way, either directly (through, for example, subscription fees) or indirectly (for example, advertising).

Many of these so-called portal sites were to become emblematic of the folly of initial attempts to commercialise the internet. The problem with portals was a lack of a firm underlying business model stemming from an almost dogged refusal of marketers to understand that the web was not simply a push medium – that people were going online and doing things, making things, and talking to one another. While many sites tried to aggregate users around expensively produced content, other non-commercial sites like forums and online games exploded in popularity. Indeed, the influx of new users into what were once the sanctum of the internet elites was bemoaned by some, who dubbed the new internet experience 'the Eternal September'.[3]

Nonetheless, the potential for users to make money for online businesses created a gold-rush mentality in the late 1990s. Billions of dollars were invested in dotcom start-up businesses that claimed to have found a way to make money online, or which in many cases made no such claims but were able to boast large numbers of (non-feepaying) users who were somehow going to turn into cash in some kind of mysterious process of transmutation. Armed only with rapidly diminishing investor capital, and devoid of proven business models, these businesses led the charge into economic oblivion.

Investment in dreams of commercialising the internet saw a rash of public companies appear on the stock market. The so-called dotcoms were typically run by young entrepreneurs who had the technical skills to develop internet sites and the contacts and audacity to acquire the venture capital that would establish themselves as a viable company. Tales of fabulous overnight wealth creation abound from the dotcom era. One online grocery retail company called WebVan, established in 1999, came to be valued at US$1.2 billion at the height of the market (German n.d.). Others were simply fantasies. Infospace, for example, debuted on the stock market with a share price of $20 a share. By early 2000 this had sky-rocketed to over $1,305 a share. This high valuation was despite a lack of any proven business model, and perhaps more strangely, upon an almost complete dearth of profits. Time, it was felt, was all that was needed to prove business models, see profits, and for dotcoms to take their place as the commercial giants of the new economy.

However, by 1999 some analysts were warning of an impending dotcom bust. Over-valued companies with little or no profits were operating on money from hopeful investors. When the money began to run out, companies disappeared, leaving large holes in the stock market. When the bust finally came in early 2000, many dotcoms vanished as fast as they had appeared. On 10 March 2000, Wall Street suffered the biggest single-day crash in its history. The crash wiped billions of dollars of value from the stock market, and the NASDAQ technology stocks index lost 78 per cent of its value (Alden, 2005).

WEB 2.0

> Web 2.0 is not a technology, it is an attitude. (O'Reilly 2005)

> 'Web 2.0' is a weird phrase. It began as the name of a conference, but the people organising the conference didn't really know what they meant by it. Mostly they thought it sounded catchy. However, 'Web 2.0' has since taken on a meaning. There are some interesting new trends on the Web, and it's the nature of a phrase like that to adhere to them. (Graham 2006)

> Nobody really knows what it means ... If Web 2.0 for you is blogs and wikis, then that is people to people. But that was what the Web was supposed to be all along. (Berners-Lee 2006)

The dotcom bust scared many investors, although a number of companies came through the bust bloodied, but alive. In the final quarter of 2001, Amazon.com turned in its first profit in some five years of operation (BBC Editorial 2002) proving that although many companies had been a bad bet, others were based on something more than speculative hype. Following the dotcom crash, numerous other companies, operating on a more cautious approach to internet commerce, also managed to survive, and some began to thrive. Perhaps the biggest factor behind the success of post-dotcom companies has been the realisation that online users are not like TV audiences. This awareness, or at least the way it has been rationalised, can be summed up by the phrase 'Web 2.0'.

According to believers in Web 2.0, Web 2.0 doesn't refer to any changes in the internet's architecture. Rather, it refers to the types of software employed and changes at the level of user practices. While Web 2.0 is often associated with internet entrepreneur Tim O'Reilly, it has more recently been recognised that the term was first used by Darcy DiNucci in 1999 to describe a new type of 'fragmentation' that would occur with the rise of mobile web devices:

> The Web has already become an almost iconic cultural reference – ubiquitous and familiar. We think we know what it is by now. The Web we know now, which loads into a window on our computer screens in essentially static screenfuls, is an embryo of the Web as we will know it in not so many years ... The first glimmerings of Web 2.0 are now beginning to appear, and we can start to see just how that embryo might develop ... The Web will be understood, not as screenfuls of text and graphics but as a transport mechanism, the ether through which interactivity happens. It will still appear on your computer screen, transformed by the video and other dynamic media made possible by the speedy connection technologies now coming down the pike. It will also appear, in different guises, on your TV set (interactive content woven seamlessly into programming and commercials), your car dashboard (maps, yellow pages,

and other traveler info), your cell phone (news, stock quotes, flight info), hand-held game machines (linking players with competitors over the Net), maybe even your microwave oven (automatically finding cooking times for the latest products). (DiNucci, 1999)

In DiNucci's somewhat science fictional future gazing, she is linking Web 2.0 to the rise of ubiquitous computing. The spectres of Mark Weiser's (1991) prescient words about the importance of context-awareness and embeddedness within the constitution of ubiquitous technologies can be felt in her vision. Weiser imagined a time in the future where computer technology would vanish into the background as we moved beyond big, clunky machines and into a world where ever-present (ubiquitous) but essentially invisible computers became as commonplace as the written word. In his vision, Weiser imagined a time when computer technologies were always available and able to provide extra information about every conceivable aspect of life – not too far different from the experience afforded by today's mobile technologies. DiNucci's focus is, however, from a designer's point of view rather than, as the term later gets recruited, from a business perspective.

Web 2.0 and business

While personalisation and content creation are fundamental concepts that have been associated with Web 2.0, the term has also been widely employed as a model for business in the post-dotcom era. For such figureheads as Tim O'Reilly, Web 2.0 has provided new ways to conceive of the internet in terms of economic value (Allen 2009: 17). In this respect, the term Web 2.0 gained currency through the O'Reilly Media Web 2.0 conference in 2004, wherein he and John Battelle defined Web 2.0 as a platform in which customers play an active role in building one's business. In doing this, they were building on ideas that had been gaining currency since the dotcom crash. O'Reilly's language and position epitomises the shift of focus away from conceiving the internet as a technological space and, instead, towards it being embedded within the social (and, in O'Reilly's case, with particular focus upon the commercial).

In recalling why O'Reilly and his associates used the term Web 2.0, O'Reilly harkens back to the dotcom crash and notes it as a 'turning point for the web' (2005). He and his colleagues felt that the crash had weeded out the bad business models, and through some kind of Darwinian process the fittest had survived, and new businesses were starting up. 'Could it be', asked O'Reilly in a 2005 post to his website, 'that the dotcom collapse marked some kind of turning point for the web, such that a call to action such as "Web 2.0" might make sense?'

O'Reilly's concept of Web 2.0 indicates that business in this new internet age is tightly related to active, engaged internet users noting that '*(n)etwork effects from user contributions are the key to market dominance in the Web 2.0 era*' (O'Reilly 2005; original emphasis). Hints of this shift towards recognising the importance of internet users – cast as customers – had begun appearing as early as 1997. As previously mentioned, Hagel's *Net Gain* first extolled the virtues of engaging with users, and was followed in 1999 by a website (later published as a book in 2000) called *The Cluetrain Manifesto*, which consists of 95 short essays or 'theses' that argue that the real power of the web is in connecting businesses with their clients. One of the key ideas from this book is that:

> ... markets are conversations. Their members communicate in language that is natural, open, honest, direct, funny and often shocking. Whether explaining or complaining, joking or serious, the human voice is unmistakably genuine. It can't be faked. (Levine et al. 2000: xi)

Signposting the already emergent movement of user created content (UCC), the authors essentially argued that such activities could be 'harnessed' to create value for businesses, a point reiterated six years later by O'Reilly. Here we can begin to see the emergence of a complex relationship between the creative and communicative practices of internet users and corporations who were interested in ways of harnessing online activities for profit.

Web 2.0 and creative production

Web 2.0 encapsulates the idea of making it easy for anyone to publish information on the internet: this is clearly linked to the new ways Web 2.0 was to work as a business. This idea encapsulates the transition from Web 1.0, which was all about reading or watching content, to Web 2.0, which is much more concerned with providing users with the means for producing and distributing content.

However, as Tim Berners-Lee's quote at the beginning of this section aptly signals, the rhetoric behind the so-called Web 2.0 revolution can be seen as an extension of the original designer's intentions. Reflecting this, early versions of web browsers like Netscape Navigator included web page editors that allowed people to make web pages, although the processes involved in getting these online were not for the faint hearted. In a fascinating devolution of technology, such features were first separated into different versions of the applications and then discontinued altogether.

Under the 'read' model of Web 1.0, if you wanted to provide information online you would need to create your own website. This generally required a lot of technical knowledge, and may have required you to run your own web server, which was a fairly daunting technical task. The Web 2.0 model sees the computer take over the task of managing technical details of formatting and presentation, allowing the user to focus on the production of content. Blogs, for example, provide a way for users to publish information online with few more technical skills than are required to use a web browser and type at a keyboard. Thus, Web 2.0 makes creating content vastly less complicated, and this, in turn, leads to much more content being put online as the technical barriers to creation are removed. Once content could readily be created by just about any user, the technological prerequisites were met for the emergence of social network sites (SNSs; see Chapter 3 for details).

For Ethan Zuckerman, in his ETech paper entitled the *Cute Cat Theory of Digital Activism*, 'Web 1.0 was invented to allow physicists to share research papers and Web 2.0 was created to allow people to share pictures of cute cats' (2008). While this somewhat facetious comment could be read in light of the shift towards experiencing and conceptualising the internet as a social space, it also highlights that, behind the oft-banal activities of users, new forms of affective sharing and communities are emerging. As Zuckerman observes, while Web 2.0 'was designed for mundane uses, it can be extremely powerful in the hands of digital activists, especially those in environments where free speech is limited' (2008). But for others such as Lovink, this 'cute cat' phenomenon is part of a simplification of the 'social' in which all journalism becomes a series of secondary references and divisions (2012: 4).

However, we could say that the personalisation of technology had been occurring long before Web 2.0, mobile media and the 'cute cat' phenomenon. Indeed, countries such as Japan have excelled globally in their ability to spearhead the 'personal technologies' revolution from the Sony Walkman onwards. Mizuko Ito (2005), for example, argues that it is the notion of the 'personal' – along with pedestrian and portable – that have characterised Japanese technologies for decades (Fujimoto 2005; Okada 2005). Part of the success has been their deployment of high-level customisation, particularly apparent in what anthropologist Brian McVeigh has called 'techno-cute'; that is, the usage of the cute to make 'warm' and 'friendly' the coldness of new technologies (2000).

Given that the kinds of behaviours attributed to Web 2.0 seem to have their roots in older and well-established cultural uses of computer and media technologies, one could argue that some formulations of Web 2.0

are somewhat hindered in their understanding of the genealogies of ICTs (information and communication technologies) and especially the internet, particularly from non-Western or Anglophonic points of view (Goggin and McLelland 2009). This sentiment is shared by World Wide Web (WWW) pioneers such as Berners-Lee who define Web 2.0 as little more than a 'piece of jargon' (2006) – and he is far from alone. O'Reilly himself acknowledges that the practices that he associates with Web 2.0 are not always novel:

> But as with many areas of Web 2.0, where the '2.0-ness' is not something new, but rather a fuller realization of the true potential of the web platform, this phrase gives us a key insight into how to design applications and services for the new platform. (O'Reilly 2005)

For Australian new media theorists Anna Munster and Andrew Murphie (2009), the confusion around rhetoric to do with Web 2.0, and the type of attendant agency it affords, is due to the fact that its semantics have been misunderstood. They argue that O'Reilly got it wrong:

> Web 2.0 is not an 'is', or not only this. Web 2.0 is also a verb or, as they taught us in primary school, it's a *doing* word. Here's a list of some Web 2.0 things to do: apping, blogging, mapping, mashing, geocaching, tagging, searching, shopping, sharing, socialising and wikkiing. And the list goes on. Yet as the list goes on it becomes apparent that part of what Web 2.0 does, while doing all the things on this list and more, is colonise everything in the network. It seems that there is no part of networked thought, activity or life that is not now Web 2.0 … Anything can become or be 2.0 as long as it demonstrates or is affiliated with a certain set of qualities. A list of typical Qualities 2.0 might look something like this: dynamic, participatory, engaged, interoperable, user-centred, open, collectively intelligent and so on. Clearly an 'attitude' can go a long way. (Munster and Murphie 2009)

As Munster and Murphie note, '2.0' characteristics include 'participatory', 'dynamic' and 'user-centred' – and while these features are presented as positives that sell Web 2.0 to users and excite us with enticements of the possible futures they promise, these features are offered within the frame-work of marketing and business. This 'attitude' points to important questions about the emerging relationship between users and businesses in the new, 2.0, post-dotcom web. On the one hand, Web 2.0 promises users empower-ment by supporting a new model of media production (and consumption) that does away with the domination of production by a few. On the other hand, it threatens control and colonisation of users' social lives. In this way, Web 2.0 is a contradiction: it is simultaneously empowering and exploitative, a platform for both control and freedom. This paradox and contestation is at the heart of social media, and it is a topic we will further examine in the second half of this chapter.

USING OR BEING USED?

> The danger of participation is that there are hundreds or even thousands of potentially critical eyes watching every entry. A faulty fact will be challenged, a lie will be uncovered, plagiarism will be discovered. Cyberspace is a truth serum. (Rushkoff 1994: 36)

> The signs are growing that the once-anarchic, perhaps emancipatory internet is subject to increasing attempts to privatize, commercialise, control and profit from the activities of consumers online. (Livingstone 2005: 2–3)

The term 'user' has two connotations: controller and controlled. In computer parlance, the user is in charge of the machine. The user is in control (at least apparently) of the computer's operation – the computer seemingly does nothing unless a user clicks a mouse button or presses a key. On the other hand, within software development circles the user is often derided. When we think about users in the context of social media, and particularly within the construct of Web 2.0, which one of these categories is most applicable? Are users the controllers, who are powerful because they can create the content in stark contrast to the powerless audience of mass media, or are users the subjects of control, as their personal information and creative and cultural labour is monitored and commodified by social media companies?

These questions are phrased here as binary opposites, and as such they represent ideal positions at the extreme ends of a spectrum of different possibilities. Certainly, social media can be seen as empowering or it can be seen as a set of tools for commercialising the social, affective and creative efforts of the user. The ambient intimacy of everyday SNS practices (the way the SNS can sit idle in the background while the user works on something else, or the way that Twitter is always at hand on the mobile device but not always actively engaged with) makes it hard to pin down how much work the user is doing and how this translates to value for the social media company. Work by Banks and Humphreys (2008) in the area of game players, along with Bruns' model of the 'produser' (see Chapter 3 for detailed discussion), have attempted to provide more useful models for conceptualising the often tacit labour that accompanies contemporary media practice today.

Social media as empowering

It is tempting to look at social media as a democratic revolution in the media, and indeed it has been trumpeted as such in some of the earliest writings about the internet (Lovink 2012). At the heart of these arguments is the idea that the internet bypasses old structures of control and power – instead of a few powerful people controlling what the majority see and hear, the majority can now produce (and reproduce) media. This decentralisation of the production of media content also decentralises media control, which poses vast challenges for media companies that established their media empires based upon a monopoly over distribution. This, in turn, leads some observers to see the internet as an inherently democratising or emancipatory medium because of the way it seems to empower individuals and undermine old monopolies and systems of power.

This narrative of empowerment has a long history that pre-dates the popular internet and has its roots in the techno-utopianism of counter-culture movements of the 1960s and with libertarian ideals that are fundamentally intertwined with the political landscape of the US. Metaphors that engaged concepts such as the 'virtual frontier' invoked notions of new, open spaces that were free of the controls of an old order, a kind of 'Wild West' without the dust and guns. Given that the early development of the internet was driven largely by the US, it is hardly surprising that these ideals should hail from the cultural and political traditions of that nation. In this particular Anglophonic evolution, issues such as race and gender performativity have become key battlegrounds (Nakamura 2002). As Lisa Nakamura has so eloquently discussed, often locations such as Tokyo have become a 'default' setting for Western imaginations of the future and technology.

A number of influential commentators managed to capture people's imaginations with romantic concepts that meshed US libertarianism with 1960s alternative culture and the emergence of new technologies. John Perry Barlow, for example, presented a firmly libertarian view of the internet in his *A Cyberspace Independence Declaration* (1996), as did Douglas Rushkoff in *Cyberia* (1994). These influential works cast the internet as something that was above and beyond the reach of industrial governments, which John Perry Barlow described as 'weary giants of flesh and steel' (1996).

Adding to these romantic concepts of the internet as being beyond the reach of old power structures (understood by Barlow in true US-libertarian style primarily as governments) were claims that the technology itself was inherently democratising. It became a known 'fact' that the internet was developed to withstand nuclear attack (Chun 2006: 65), and this robustness in the face of the greatest threat known to humankind helped to elevate the internet – often referred to as cyberspace – to the sublime. This immunity to nuclear war extended beyond physical attacks and into the political realm. The internet, according to John Gilmore 'treats censorship as damage, and routes around it' (Elmer-Dewitt 1993). In this light, the internet could not be stopped, let alone tamed.

In the decade following these initial works, a great deal changed on the internet. As described above, the demographic profile of internet users changed as more and more people came online, and businesses started colonising the internet. The dotcom crash was for some a kind of proof that the internet was resistant to control. The emergence of Web 2.0 and the near simultaneous emergence of mobile internet has again raised questions about the ability of the internet to bypass conventional control and bring about social change. Some of these themes, like citizen journalism and online activism, are addressed in more detail in Chapter 3. Others are less visible, and are represented in a variety of ways, but all focus on the ways that social media empower the individual.

Certainly, it is difficult to ignore the way that social media has greatly expanded the networked individual's access to information. For the lucky ones, answers to many questions are only a Google search away (though veracity may be a little further afield). SNSs, as we will discuss in Chapter 4, provide them with access to a wider social network, allowing them to find employment or maintain social relationships that once would have died owing to distance. Networked individuals have access to a large repository of media almost at whim (YouTube, for example), and can make creative works that can be enjoyed by thousands or millions of people where once they might have been consigned to the back of a cupboard, to be discovered by relatives sometime after they had died.

On a larger scale, social media has been implicated in regime change and is playing an increasingly important role in the political: from unofficial uprisings like the Arab Spring to political campaigns. With the uprising of the Arab Spring in the Middle East, we have seen ways in which social and mobile media can be used to help mobilise new forms of politics while at the same time amplifying paradoxes around media *effects* and *affects*. For example, the control/freedom paradox of the online addressed by Chun (2006) can be seen in the recent 'liberation technology' (Diamond and Plattner 2012) rhetoric of the Arab Spring in which media can both be a site for emancipation (in the case of Egypt and Tunisia) and a reinforcing authoritarian state (Iran). Governments in some countries are becoming interested in social media as a way to engage more directly with citizens, and citizens are using social media to draw attention to local issues (Shirky 2009). We give this aspect of user participation more treatment in Chapter 4.

Social media as control

A medium that allows users to create things and develop a voice which also eludes regulation by authorities can lead to significant positive (perhaps even emancipatory) impacts in many areas of society, from the economy to politics (see Chapter 4 for a detailed discussion of the changing nature of citizen journalism through vehicles such as Twitter). On the face of it, social media gives a great deal more control back to the majority of people. Yet there are also arguments to the contrary: while social media undermines many existing media models, it also establishes new ones.

As James Beniger showed in the 1980s, computers and communications technologies were developed primarily to increase centralised management and control of industrial processes, not to diminish them. It is probably a little rash to simply dismiss this argument as irrelevant to the internet, although in the face of so many internet-led changes that seem to be undermining industrial economic structures (the music industry springs to mind), it is tempting to ignore arguments to the contrary.

Since the beginning of the industrial revolution, control has been an ongoing concern. As production sped up and more goods were produced and moved faster and in greater variety to diverse markets, increasingly sophisticated information systems were required to maintain control. Seen in this light, the evolution of digital computers is a response to the need for increased control in industrialised countries (Beniger 1986). Although Beniger was writing well before the rise of the internet – let alone social media – it is possible to extrapolate and see the rise of social media as part of the refinement in control that Beniger identified. While in some respects social media is democratising, empowering and emancipatory, it also makes us all more dependent upon the digital. Consider how 'lost' a typical teenager is without a mobile phone or access to SNSs like Facebook. For many young people today, even the idea of being without their phone or social media for a day causes great distress. This dependency makes us all more subject to the control mechanisms of the information society; to be counted, sorted and organised into groups that can be matched with products and processed as fast as materials and services can be produced and distributed.

For Andrejevic, networked social interaction moderated by SNSs, for example, are structured around a 'storable and sortable' separation between users and the means of socialising. In other words, in order to participate in an SNS, a person must create an account, and in so doing they are immediately creating online information about themselves. Because the information is digital, it can be processed and compared, allowing the owners of the SNS to create 'collections of data' that can then be repurposed by companies and marketing campaigns (Andrejevic 2011: 88). Following on from the work of Terranova on today's 'social factories', Andrejevic argues that commercial interests are 'colonising' narratives of personal self-presentation and sociality. Sonia Livingstone would appear to concur. She writes:

> [W]e must instead ask questions about how, and with what consequences, it has come about that all social situations (whether at home or work, in public or in private, at school or out shopping) are now, simultaneously, mediated spaces, thereby constituting their participants inevitably as both family, workers, public or communities and as audiences, consumers or users? (2005: 25–6)

Cast in this light, social media can be seen as a step in increasing the control afforded by the information technologies. This point becomes clearer if we compare social media with television, and consider how much more useful consumer information can be gathered relatively easily. While television provided an important means for product makers to connect with audience through advertising, television also suffered from a number of shortcomings. Under a broadcast model, for example, nobody can tell what television station is being watched at any one time. Broadcast companies pay top dollar to media ratings companies like ACNielsen who go to extraordinary lengths to determine ratings for television programmes. Broadcasters simply don't know who is watching their channels without polling the audience. Unless somebody is watching you from across the street, you can be completely certain that when you are watching a broadcast TV programme, you are the only person who knows you're watching it.

On the internet, however, every time you sit down at your computer and access a website, your activity is instantly recorded by multiple sources – if not your ISP, then at the very least, the website that is receiving your request, and generally by a much more complex array of monitoring systems that help website owners and search companies develop a profile of each individual's online habits. No matter how little information you provide to sites and services (and many people provide quite a lot), the mere fact you are connected to the internet immediately compromises your privacy. People who wish to maintain their privacy online must go to significant lengths to do so, and require a level of technical proficiency that eludes most internet users. When seen in this light, the internet seems to be as much an advance in control as an empowerment of the user.

The fact that everything is logged and available for analysis opens up a new and valuable source of information for companies – very precise information about the browsing habits of internet users, which in turn allows for a much, much greater targeting of advertising and the prospect of direct sales to the consumer, or simply the sale of collected information about users to other parties. Instead of undermining central authority and power, this seems to be doing the opposite. The processes of control are now beginning to move further into our private lives, and users and their cultural and interpersonal activities are being monitored, regulated and managed like never before.

In Wendy Chun's (2006) excellent book on the internet, the dichotomy of control and freedom are presented as a paradox. Chun argues that the meaning of freedom has gradually been shifted to incorporate control as an implicit precondition. In other words, if you want freedom, then you have to submit to control. This apparent contradiction makes a strange kind of sense in a post-9/11 world where phantom terrorists lurk in every airport terminal. According to this logic, there can be no greater threat to individual freedom than death, and the only thing standing between us and death at the hands of a terrorist is often control applied through surveillance – full-body scanners, constant monitoring through security cameras, the tightly regimented processing of people.

Conversely, our sense of freedom is realised through a sense of control because the more control one has, the argument goes, the more freedom you have to do what you want. Here we return to the earlier point mentioned near the beginning of this section about users, and the ambiguity of the term. The user is understood as a powerful individual, and this notion is reinforced in information technology and the internet all the time. Microsoft's slogan 'Where do you want to go today?' embraces the notion of the all-powerful user who is in absolute control of his or her destiny within the online environment.

As Chun points out, this draws upon earlier conceptions of cyberspace as being a place beyond space (as we noted above), and also draws upon popular representations of cyberspace from fiction which preceded and accompanied the development of the internet. From William Gibson's cyberpunk novels and Neal Stephenson's *Snow Crash* to a raft of thematically similar books and films, images of cyberspace have been constructed as a place where the individual is in control. From the utopian holodeck of *Star Trek: The Next Generation* to the dystopian virtual reality that featured as a central plot device in the Wachowski Brothers' *Matrix*, virtual online cyberspaces have been represented as a place where the user exerts control over his or her destiny by knowing or learning how to control their online environment.

SNSs, as one example of Web 2.0 applications, also place the user at the centre of their own universe, a platform on which to stand to engage with and control their online space. As discussed above, underlying this so-called user-centred media is the fact that the data is then mined and sold to advertisers (Vaidhyanathan 2011; Lovink 2012; boyd and Crawford 2012). Consider that Facebook has some 800 million subscribers at the time of writing, and yet each and every one of these subscribers (users) has a network of friends in which they are the central nodes that organises everything else. The user can switch off unwanted contacts, send messages out to hundreds (or millions, just as easily), all the while developing the illusion of freedom through control. This isn't just any space that the user is (apparently) controlling, it is not even cyberspace; it is their own 'personal' space. YouTube places *you* at the centre of the universe, and MySpace, as this SNS so helpfully points out, creates an online space that is supposedly *mine*.

However, as Chun argues, it is in the interests of the companies behind these services to foster and develop the illusion of control. Providing users with a certain kind of control (the ability to create profiles and interact with others and produce cultural objects), all mediated within the company's platform, actually establishes broader economic and political controls over the whole system. We have used the term 'platform' here a couple of times to draw attention to another way of thinking about Web 2.0. Tarleton Gillespie notes that a platform has a number of definitions in English language, which together suggest 'a progressive and egalitarian arrangement, lifting up those who stand upon it' (Gillespie 2010: 350). When applied to Web 2.0 applications such as YouTube, Facebook or Twitter, the term suggests that the role of the company is impartial – they are just there to provide a platform that users can stand on and be treated as equals.

The principles of the platform are enshrined in Facebook's 10 principles that, at the time of writing, contain the word 'free' or 'freedom' no less than 14 times (http://www.facebook.com/principles.php). Facebook's role as an open, free conduit for users to become empowered through their networked agency is also reinforced through its mission statement, which reads in part: 'to give people the power to share and make the world more open and connected' (www.facebook.com/facebook). Supposedly, Facebook is simply the catalyst that makes these things possible. It is a wonder, then, that Facebook should have been at the forefront of debates about privacy and intellectual property. Given that many of its changes have given few rights to their users, and in many cases have appeared to be self-serving rather than user-empowering;

arguments that social media are purely about putting the user in control need to be taken with more than just a grain of salt.

While the platform metaphor seems to support the empowerment of the user, it also plays another role, echoing Chun's paradoxical alignment of freedom and control. As we discussed above, Web 2.0 companies – those that emerged after the dotcom bust, or which rode it out – are companies that recognise the importance of and value of a user's online practices, and use those practices to enhance their businesses. This works for users, because it means there are many services available that are cheap or free. Writing a blog, putting videos online, developing software, creating or participating in online communities – all these activities are free, given away by companies whose actual motivations are less clear. What does an SNS like YouTube, Facebook or a search engine company like Google get in return for their apparently altruistic motives? The answer, of course, is control.

Google is a prime example of a company that has embraced (or helped define) the Web 2.0 platform mantra. As a search engine company, Google's most prominent service is its almost universally known search page – a web page that's incredibly simple given the behemoth that lies behind it. Every day Google's computers index content on the internet, creating a massive searchable database of most of the pages on the web. This vast database is then provided to us via the Google homepage, or directly within our browser software, and provides us with virtually instant access to many topics, and with a little effort, many more beyond. Yet for all this, Google does not charge its users a cent. The service is free.

Google's revenue stream is drawn primarily from its advertising business. When you type in a search term like 'price of tulips', Google's AdWords advertising engine will attempt to connect your search term with terms that advertisers have purchased. If a match is found, you will not only get your search results but also a list of results directing you to advertisers – in this case, mainly florists. Google is at pains to keep this part of their business separate from the search business. They don't try to integrate the advertisements into the actual search results, and they do not allow anyone to pay money to have their sites appear at the top of search results. Google's search algorithms – the methods they use to locate and present relevant information – are sacrosanct. The reason for this is quite simple: if the search engine becomes less effective, users will start using other engines, and that will cost Google market share. So, while Google's Adwords advertisements are presented in strategic places on search results pages, Google uses various techniques to visually separate them from the list of unpaid search results.

The main point here is that Google's business model is ostensibly about users. Google's 'about' page says that the number one thing they know to be true is 'focus on the user and all else will follow' (www.google.com/intl/en/about/). However, as Siva Vaidhyanathan notes in *The Googlization of Everything*, 'we are not Google's customers: we are its product' (2011: 3). Here Vaidhyanathan echoes Chun's position – that the publicly touted importance of Google as a platform for the user lies within a more fundamental Web 2.0 business model where *users* are actually the source of value, not the information on the web that Google indexes. When we search on Google, Google builds profiles that match search terms with sites visited. Websites install Google Analytics, which allows them to quickly and easily see who is visiting their pages, but also allows Google to see where people are going. This is generally aggregated – Google doesn't care so much where you went today, but does care where 'you all' went today.

More than that, companies like Google are engaging in a process that might be seen as horizontal integration. In traditional hierarchical markets (lemonade manufacturers, say), horizontal integration is where one company buys out its competitors and by so doing is able to corner the market for lemonade. Google's purchases of YouTube and its integration of other services like Gmail into one happy family doesn't immediately appear to be horizontal integration because all the companies it is buying are all doing different things: YouTube serves video, Gmail is an online email application, Google is a search engine and Google+ is a social network tool. If, however, we accept Vaidhyanathan's argument, that users are Google's product, then critically, the same could be said for the sites. YouTube is a platform creating users, as is Gmail, as is Google+. Therefore, Google's purchase of YouTube allowed them to horizontally integrate, dominating not the streaming video market but the user-as-commodity market.

CONCLUSION

Web 2.0 is a notion that encapsulates a lot more than the idea that users are important, or that markets are conversations. It is a philosophy of doing business in the online environment and it is a response to the challenges of control in a networked society where many of the structures established by industrial societies are not always as effective. According to this philosophy, Web 2.0 is the more advanced, updated, better version of Web 1.0. What's updated and improved here is not the technical architecture of the web itself, but the way that business has come to think about the web, and most importantly, the ability of business to exert control in an environment which had previously been seemingly resistant to it.

The changes said to be part of Web 2.0 are sold to users as desirable primarily because they apparently increase users' control over their environments: freedom through control. The changes improve the agency of the networked individual, and through doing this apparently give us all more freedom. However, while Web 2.0 can be regarded as internet companies embracing the user and giving them more control over what they can do online, it can also be regarded as a way for the same companies to gain more control over their operating environments by building better knowledge of their users. The real revolution encompassed by Web 2.0 is a revolution in thinking, where internet companies have finally come up with a way of understanding the internet and working out effective methods for using it as a technology of control in the networked society.

Here we should go back to one of the points we made earlier. The tensions between control and freedom should not be treated as absolute positions, where you take a side and fight it out to the end. Instead, these represent extreme ends of a spectrum in which complex interactions play out. Sometimes social media is empowering, and may work very effectively to increase a user's agency and ability to control and interact with their environment. Other times social media can be controlling, providing significant financial benefits to the social media company but little or no compensation to the user for their time and energy. Most often social media is both controlling and empowering at the same time, in an uneasy relationship where a certain amount of exploitation is negotiated as the price for a certain amount of empowerment. In the following chapters we will explore some of these themes further.

NOTES

1 The use of a number like 1.0 is something adopted from computer programming practice. When a computer program was finished, it was given a version number – version 1.0 for the first final, complete version of the software. As the software was further developed other versions would be given a number like 1.1 or 1.2 to indicate that they represented minor developments. When the software underwent a major overhaul, it might be given a whole new version number to indicate the significance of the update – version 1.5 might be upgraded to version 2.0, for example. During the 1980s, this quickly became part of the marketing strategy for software, with companies offering up new versions

of software regularly, exhorting their users to continue buying new software so they could take advantage of the latest features.

2 Although it's worth noting that Netscape itself ended up losing market share to Microsoft's Internet Explorer and eventually folded, only to be reborn as project Phoenix, which due to trademark issues ended up being renamed Firefox.

3 The Eternal September – the rapid growth of internet users mirrored experiences on forums each year when new people started at college in the northern hemisphere. The influx of new users created problems within the social fabric of online forums and each year took weeks in which the relatively small number of 'newbies' were initiated into the correct modes of behaviour. Massive influxes of new internet users, particularly from AOL, overwhelmed these social systems, leading to the Eternal September.

3 Social network sites

What makes social network sites unique is not that they allow individuals to meet strangers, but rather that they enable users to articulate and make visible their social networks. (boyd and Ellison 2007)

[S]ocial networking sites don't publicise community, they privatise it. (Andrejevic 2011: 97)

Social media is increasingly infiltrating everyday media practices. As we witness the rise of smartphones that allow users to move ambiently between social media like Facebook and Twitter at all times of the day, how we define social network sites (SNSs) is changing. As a series of cultural practices and artefacts that are both commercial and cultural, SNSs are becoming an integral part of identity, social and political management. But does this pervasiveness of SNS result in a flattening in definitions of the 'social' as some critics might suggest (Lovink 2012)? What does the ubiquitous nature of social media, especially as it becomes incorporated with mobile and locative media, say about contemporary media practice? Are SNSs transforming notions of publicness, privacy and intimacy (boyd 2011)? Or are the changes more dynamic and complex than previously theorised? Can alternative social media practices be formed in the face of monopolies such as Facebook (Lovink 2012)?

SNSs are at the interface between people and social media. These sites represent some of the most well-known and most highly valued brands (in market, if not social terms) on the internet today. For many the 'internet' is synonymous with SNSs. Names such as Facebook, Qzone, Twitter, Habbo, Renren and Badoo boast millions of online users who use these services to build connections with other people, to stay in touch, to find support and answers to questions, to reinforce common ideas and values, to share news and other information, and to be entertained. These sites have become exemplars of the Web 2.0 ethos and the shift in focus from users as audiences to users as networked publics that we identified in Chapter 2. In many ways

SNSs represent the intersection of networked publics and business interests, although, as we will see below, this is by no means a perfect fit.

In this chapter we want to develop an understanding of SNSs that goes beyond the popular and stereotyped notions of SNSs as being an Anglophonic domain populated by under-25s engaging in banal conversations about what they got up to on the weekend. Instead, we present SNSs as a global phenomenon that is engaging people from broad demographics in a variety of ways. Most importantly, we are interested in the ways that SNSs provide places for the construction and maintenance of relationships between people. Building on the themes we established in Chapter 2, and will expand upon in Chapter 4 (Web 2.0, networked publics, produsage and playbour), we look at how SNSs are deeply embedded within offline contexts, and support many kinds of activities which have very real social, economic, political and cultural consequences.

In the first part of this chapter we explore research that reveals the complexity that lies behind SNSs. Then we examine how SNSs have developed in non-Anglophonic contexts, and explore some of the ways that these contexts challenge Anglocentric understandings of social networks. In this section we consider how different groups that cut across demographic, cultural and social boundaries are using social networks, casting doubt over the persistent stereotypes and memes about online relations that still get presented in many forums, especially the mainstream media.

The final part of this chapter will review some of the ways that SNSs are being researched, to provide a broad overview of the main themes and topics in what is becoming a very closely studied phenomenon. We will end the chapter with a summary of the key points we have covered. But before we begin with the deeper analysis, let us begin with a working definition of SNSs.

DEFINING SOCIAL NETWORK SITES

There are dozens if not hundreds of sites that meet the functional definition of an SNS (which is, at its most fundamental level, a site that allows users to create some kind of online presence and articulate that with others). SNSs come in a range of shapes and sizes, from the behemoth that is Facebook, which at the time of writing claims it has over 800 million subscribers, to the small and niche-like WriteAPrisoner.com, a US-based SNS that allows pen-pal-like communications with the outside world, with the goal of easing prisoner's transition from jail back into the community.

In attempting to define social network sites, it is useful to note boyd and Ellison's (2007) comment that the terms 'network' and 'networking' are often used interchangeably in critical literature. boyd and Ellison prefer the use of the term 'network' because, for them, networking implies the initiation of relationships by strangers. Consider, for example, a business *networking* event, where the point of the event is for people who have certain interests to meet other people who also share those interests. Here the emphasis is on the construction of new relationships. SNSs, while supporting this kind of relationship construction, are more frequently used by people to maintain existing relationships, and so boyd and Ellison elect to use the term 'social *network* site' to emphasise their role in maintenance of relationships that in many cases exist in offline as well as online contexts. We will return to this point later in the chapter.

At the core of social network sites is the construction of social networks that are enabled and enhanced by the internet. To date, boyd and Ellison's definition of SNS has been the most accurate. SNS are:

> web-based services that allow individuals to (1) construct a public or semi-public profile within a bounded system, (2) articulate a list of other users with whom they share a connection, and (3) view and traverse their list of connections and those made by others within the system. (boyd and Ellison 2007)

Most social network sites share a number of common features such as profiles, lists of connections, comments and private messaging. Profiles are how users identify themselves to the social media site, and usually contain a range of information about the user, including a name (and sometimes a screen name), email address (which is often kept hidden), birth date and other biographical information. Many sites also encourage users to upload a photo for use in their profiles. This information helps to build social networks and allows for site features like annual birthday reminders but also has clear implications for users' privacy. Some sites make their users' profiles publicly available, while others keep profiles hidden, only revealing them to other users of the SNS based on their relationship with the profile's owner.

A list of connections or relationships with other users of the SNS – sometimes called 'friends', although as boyd and Ellison point out, people in these lists may not actually be considered friends by the user – allows individuals to assert relationships with other individuals on the network. How these links are created depends on the site. For some SNSs, like Twitter, connections can be made unilaterally by one party, and a distinction is made between those people a user has linked to, and people who have linked to the user. In Twitter these incoming/outgoing links are distinguished by the terms 'followers' and 'following'. Other SNSs, such as LinkedIn, require the link to be agreed to by both parties. Most SNSs also have ways of enabling users to link with contacts who are not signed up to the service, usually by dispatching an email to the other party which contains instructions on how to sign up for the SNS so they can accept the connection. This is one mechanism through which SNS can increase their subscriber base.

Comments, status updates and private messages allow communication between people on the network. The communication may be used like instant messaging (real-time conversations), may be a question inviting a response ('Does anyone know what's going on with the traffic this morning?') or may simply be a statement ('Just had lunch, tuna is great!') that is not intended to provoke a response but serves to keep an individual's social network alive by reminding others in the network that the individual is still there (Crawford 2010).

There are many dozens of SNSs, with some based around a theme, while others have no theme at all, other than offering a way for people to make connections. For example, LinkedIn is themed around people's working and business relationships, and Flixster is for developing social networks based around films. On the other hand, Facebook, Twitter and Google+ have no central organising theme (although Facebook did start as a site for US college students). Some sites aim to cater for specific social groups (BlackPlanet for African-American users; OUTeverywhere for lesbian/gay/bisexual/trans-sexual users, for example), although many do not. Even amongst sites that do not target any particular group some level of social differentiation does seem to have occurred. For example, in the US at least, LinkedIn has an older demographic than MySpace (Hampton et al. 2011), and Orkut is popular in Brazil and India (even though the service is based in the US). As we will discuss below, this connection of SNSs with national identity incorporates public displays of intimacy that help to establish and reinforce connections in an online environment, reflecting underlying influences in the way people use social networks that are not immediately visible.

COMMUNITIES AND NETWORKS

Despite social media being a relatively recent phenomenon, research into people using network technologies to communicate with others pre-dates the development of social media by decades. From the 1980s, pioneers like Barry Wellman were already engaging with questions about the nature of sociality within what was generally referred to as 'computer-mediated communication'. This included internet-based networks, but also bulletin board systems and networked work places. While one theme in this early work suggested that online interaction was a poor substitute for face-to-face communication (often based on workplace-based studies), others recognised that some people were using the networks for more social activities.

This section provides an overview of the discipline of internet studies, which looks at the subject of what people do online, what kinds of structures are re-mediated and what kind of structures are new. We will look at the 'ethnographic turn' that has become increasingly apparent in internet studies since the late 1990s and how debate has emerged in this discipline around the question of whether online interactions are best described as communities or networks.

Virtual communities

Back in 1993, Howard Rheingold popularised the idea of virtual communities in his book by the same name (and subtitled, importantly, 'Homesteading on the Electronic Frontier'). Rheingold's book examined his experiences with an early online community called the WELL, a pre-internet community based around Northern Californian new age ideologies. The WELL – an acronym for Whole Earth Lectronic Link – was a computer bulletin board maintained by a group of alternative lifestyle users who also produced the Whole Earth Catalog. Stewart Brand, editor of the catalogue and founder of the WELL, coined the aphorism 'information wants to be free' (Clarke 2000).

Rheingold's work popularised the notion of online communities, and fed into emerging media interest in the fledgling internet. On one side of what Wellman and Gulia (1999) have described as a Manichaean and unscholarly debate were those who derided the idea of online communities as mere escapism, and yet further evidence of the decay of society and social relations. Here, the image that was constructed was of a socially awkward computer nerd, sitting in his basement engaged in a fantasy world that further removed him from reality and social connections. Castells points out that these negative images of online communication fed into existing pessimistic narratives about the loss of community in the modern suburb or megacity (2001: 125).

Others, like Rheingold, saw potential in these online environments to create new kinds of communities that could reinvigorate public discussion and debate. Instead of seeing these networks as socially isolating, many argued that the internet created a new space for social interaction and democratic participation, establishing some of the basis for claims about the internet as an empowering medium, as discussed in Chapter 2. For others still, this online or virtual construction of social spaces was reminiscent of what Ray Oldenburg (1989) had described as 'great good places' or 'third places'. Such places exist outside the home and work, and are places where conversation is the main activity, positions are levelled (for example, the boss/worker relationship is left at the door when entering the third place) and the mood is generally playful. Most importantly, they are places that are readily accessible to everyone. A number of scholars (Kendall 2002; Soukup 2006) have argued that online spaces meet Oldenburg's criteria for third places, and it is a theme we will return to in Chapter 6 when considering the social environments constructed by social media games.

Some, like Sherry Turkle (1984, 1995), also argued that these spaces opened up opportunities for experimentation with new forms of identity, and pointed to the ways that online communication had the potential to free the individual from his or her body, allowing them to play in the realm of their imagination. This, in turn, allowed the playful exploration of concepts like gender. The online environment appeared to be a space which acted like a playground for identity, although some of the best work in this area still acknowledged the importance of offline factors (Turkle 1995; Baym 1998). However, in Turkle's later work, *Alone Together*, she did an about-face in terms of her celebration of the online.

These studies were conducted in the early days of the internet and often referred to people's own journeys through online communication environments. However, as larger numbers of people started joining the internet and commercialisation and dotcom excitement began to kick in, the character of these early environments began to change.

Networked communities

As the number of people using the internet began to burgeon in the mid-1990s, internet researchers had more opportunity to study online communities. Researchers began to discuss and emphasise the continuity of offline relationships and behaviours of users over discontinuity, amplifying the importance of social context. While a great deal of research has been done into online communities over the years, it is difficult to ignore the contribution of certain key scholars. Wellman conducted some of the first studies into the ways people used information technologies, and was one of the first people to argue for the importance of offline factors in online communication.

In one study Wellman, along with his colleagues, studied the ways that computer scientists working in universities used computer networks as part of both their work and social interaction. One of the key findings was that people communicated more depending on how strong their offline ties were. People who were already friends, or who had developed relationships with each other through work, communicated with each other more often on these networks (Haythornthwaite and Wellman 1998). The findings of this and other studies led Wellman to argue for more robust models of understanding online communities where offline factors were recognised as having an important role in online communication. Wellman and Haythornthwaite brought these perspectives together with other research in their edited collection *The Internet in Everyday Life* (2002).

The recognition that online experiences were grounded in real-world settings led to what could be termed an 'ethnographic shift' in internet studies. A good example of the ethnographic shift in internet studies is reflected in Daniel Miller and Don Slater's (2001) study, which looked at the use of the internet by Trinidadians. Their focus went beyond the online behaviours of Trinidadians to engage with the way in which internet use is contextualised with other (offline) cultural activities. Rather than attempting to generalise their study to describe all internet behaviour, Miller and Slater concerned themselves only with explaining the specific instance of internet use that their study focused on.

Unlike earlier studies of online communities, which typically started by constructing the online environment as a novel communicative space, Miller and Slater saw geographical place and the offline social world of their users as an extremely important consideration in their attempts to understand Trinidadian use of the internet. They describe their approach as 'one that sees it [the internet] embedded in a specific place, which it also transforms' (Miller and Slater 2001: 21). In this way, the internet shapes, and is shaped by, the cultural context in which it is performed. Miller and Slater found that being Trinidadian was an important factor in how and why people in Trinidad went online. Furthermore, they discovered in some cases that the online environment provided a space where people could be Trinidadian.

A key facet of these new internet community studies was the recognition that the internet is not one monolithic or homogeneous communication technology. Instead, the internet is presented as an unbounded object, which escapes a single all-encompassing definition. Unlike a mass media subject such as television, the internet is not understood as representing a totality. From this perspective, the internet is defined by an ongoing process of meaning making, a process through which the internet is socially constructed through its use. Moreover, in this understanding there is not one definition of the internet but many, depending on the context of the people who use the internet and the context of that use. Miller and Slater, for example, argued that the internet must be 'disaggregated', emphasising that it is important:

> not to look at a monolithic medium called 'the Internet', but rather at a range of practices, software and hardware technologies, modes of representation and interaction that may or may not be interrelated by participants, machines or programs (indeed they may not all take place at a computer). (Miller and Slater 2001: 14)

Miller and Slater describe the internet as both a 'symbolic totality' (as people do refer to an entity called 'the internet') as well as a 'practical multiplicity' – because one individual's definition of the internet might be radically different to another's (2001: 16). Christine Hine, another leading researcher who uses an ethnographic approach to the study of internet communities, reinforces this by pointing out that while common parlance might invoke the phrase 'the internet' as a single technological object, the actual meaning of 'internet' can be quite different depending on who is speaking and who is being spoken to. For example, she refers to the variety of different attitudes and ideas about the internet reflected by the students in her undergraduate classes (Hine 1998: 30).

Following her own interests in studying the internet from an ethnographic perspective, Hine has argued that the internet can be treated as both culture and a cultural artefact (1998). She points out that the notion of 'the internet' has meaning attached to it through a process of social negotiation. For example, the parents of grown children may have internet access, but not know what to do with it. However, when one of their children moves interstate or overseas, email may become an important method for maintaining contact. And when a baby is born in a family, a family member sets up a website with digital photographs of the new baby, and so the internet acquires meaning again, this time as represented through the web.

Manuel Castells picks up this theme and connects it back to his well-known overarching metaphor of the networked society. Castells points out that in studies such as Wellman's early work, and the Pew Internet and American Life Project, internet use is revealed as instrumental to the activities of everyday life. Earlier characterisations of 'virtual communities', then, needed to be reconsidered to de-emphasise the virtual and emphasise the connectedness of activities both online and offline.

Both Wellman and Castells argue that while the family still forms the basis for many of the strongest social ties in people's lives, other strong ties are formed through activities like work or play, and these ties may not necessarily be based on geographic proximity. We may work with people who live hours away from us in the modern city, but we develop ties with them based on shared knowledge and experience, and the internet allows us to maintain these relationships over distance. These relationships take on the character of networks in that each of us is connected to others by ties that, if mapped out, would resemble a map of a computer or telephone network.

This does not mean that these ties between people are always strong, but as Castells points out, just because a tie is weak does not mean that it is not important. People coming together in an online forum to discuss a topic of shared interest may come to know one another through their posts, but never meeting in real life or knowing the real person means these are weak ties. However, dismissing these 'weak ties' as unimportant is clearly a mistake, as Clay Shirky demonstrates in telling the story of a lost Motorola Razr phone (2008). In this example of the power of social networks, Shirky relates the story of how a lost phone that had been taken by a passerby was recovered through the activities of an online community. The links between the protagonist in this story and the community could be characterised as weak – he didn't know any of the people who helped him recover the phone – but the weakness of the relationships did not make the relationships ineffectual.

Wellman has pointed out that in many modern societies, a phenomenon he calls 'networked individualism' has arisen; that is, individuals build networks to solve problems, make decisions or get support. The internet has vastly extended these networks so that they are no longer constrained by space. This change moves people away from traditional geographically bounded social groups – neighbourhoods, for example – and towards 'sparsely-knit and loosely-bounded networks' (Wellman 2003). For Castells, networked individualism is part of the networked society, rather than the internet *per se*, but can be supported and augmented by the internet to produce 'new patterns of sociability based on individualism' (Castells 2001: 130). To illustrate this, ask yourself a question: if you are thinking of buying something – let's say a new car – do you first get advice from a neighbour or someone you work with, or do you Google it? If the answer is the latter, then you're engaging in networked individualism.

Networked publics

With the rise of the SNS, questions about the nature of online community have again become a topic of interest. danah boyd has reworked the idea of networked communities within the SNS to describe networked 'publics' as an extension (but not necessarily an alternative) to the word 'communities'. When we speak of '*the* public', we are in fact talking about a collection of publics. A public, on the other hand is a bounded collective of individuals who have come together under a common set of principles, affinities or beliefs that bind and define the public – 'a relation among strangers' (Warner 2002). The public forms a single new entity that can be a social actor. There is also the assumption that these publics are open and designed for participation by everyone; they are not 'privates', although, because they are bounded, they necessarily have implicit rules which define what is considered part of that public, and what is not.

According to boyd, networked publics are:

> publics that are restructured by networked technologies. As such, they are simultaneously (1) the space constructed through networked technologies and (2) the imagined collective that emerges as a result of the intersection of people, technology, and practice. (2011: 39)

There are two fundamental components outlined here that are worth reiterating: networked publics are both spaces *and* groups of people who are connected through practice and technology. They are 'simultaneously a space and a collection of people' (boyd 2011: 41). Importantly, boyd argues that these publics are not just networked because they are linked together by the technology, but they are transformed and restructured by networked media. SNSs are examples of online technologies that support the production and reproduction of networked publics. As boyd notes, there are three key dynamics in SNSs: invisible audiences, collapsed contexts, and the blurring of public and private (2011: 49). In examining the transformation of publics, she observes that 'the affordances of networked publics rework publics more generally and the dynamics that emerge leak from being factors in specific settings to being core to everyday realities' (p. 53). In the pervasiveness of networked publics, boyd perceives erosions of physical barriers while, at the same time, 'many people feel unmotivated to interact with distant strangers' (p. 53). In sum, in networked publics, 'attention becomes a commodity' (p. 53).

While the notion of networked publics has considerable overlap with Castells' concepts of a networked community, networked publics differs primarily in its use of the idea of 'publics' rather than 'communities' as the organising metaphor for conceptualising online users. This is a useful alternative, because it allows us to drop the cultural associations caused by that term, a problem that Castells himself is keen to avoid (2001: 127).

NETWORKS OR COMMUNITIES?

There is still healthy debate in the scholarly discourse about the nature of the social structures that are enabled by network technologies. While Castells and others have moved away from the idea of online communities, and embraced the network metaphor, others argue for the value of understanding networked sociability as a kind of community.

The term 'community' is complicated and contested. There are a variety of definitions that make it difficult to use without also accepting the intellectual baggage that comes with them. This is why some, like Castells, prefer to avoid the term altogether. Others have persevered, with interesting results. Celia Pearce has attempted to sidestep some of the baggage by drawing on German sociologist Ferdinand Tönnies' definition of community (*Gemeinschaft*) as 'an association of individuals with a collective will that is enacted through individual effort' (2009: 5). Pearce notes that 'a community of practice is defined as a group of individuals who engage in a process of collective learning and maintain a common identity defined by a shared domain of interest or activity' (2009: 5). One of the key factors in making and maintaining a community is social capital. The concept of social capital requires a few paragraphs to explain, but it is important so it's worth a minor detour.

The term 'social capital' is used by Pierre Bourdieu (1984 [1979]) in his widely read work *Distinction: A Social Critique of the Judgement of Taste*. Bourdieu was interested in taste and how taste becomes naturalised in people. In other words, Bourdieu wanted to know what societal mechanisms led to a person from one kind of background enjoying caviar and opera, while someone else likes fried chips and hard rock music. These tastes are naturalised so that people don't even know why they like them, or how they came to like them – it just seems 'natural' for them to feel such responses. For Bourdieu, capital was a form of 'knowledge' that helped produce and naturalise taste.

To explore this, Bourdieu interviewed 1,200 French people from varying class backgrounds about their tastes in art, music and popular culture. As a result of this research, Bourdieu deployed his concept of capital to discuss what he saw as three significant kinds of capital that influenced people's taste: cultural (informed by education and upbringing), social (community and networks), and economic. These factors, along with the individual's own 'habitus' (the regulatory patterns of everyday life and everyday practices), were the contributing factors in determining one's identification with a particular lifestyle niche.

Bourdieu's concept of 'social capital' took on new significance when it was reworked by James Coleman (1988) to infer a more ego-centred concept. Social capital was then redefined by Robert Putnam as part of his savage exposé on the declining role of community and social welfare in the US in *Bowling Alone* (2000). Here Putnam characterised social capital as societal-orientated activity based upon notions of trust and reciprocity. Social capital, therefore, can be seen as an integral component in the sustainability of online communities. Reflecting upon the literature about social capital from Pierre Bourdieu onwards, Ellison et al. note that an SNS such as Facebook:

> facilitates specific types of connections between people that can generate social capital ... SNSs are continuously reshaping our social networks and the communication practices we use to maintain them, and thus constitute a vibrant, important, and challenging context for studying communication practices and their social capital outcomes. (2011: 141)

In his reworking of the concept of SNS as community, Parks argues that Rheingold's depiction of the virtual community may find a new home in SNSs (Parks 2011). Reviewing various definitions of community, he determined that there are five characteristics that constitute a virtual community. Each of these characteristics are difficult to measure, so Parks derived three affordances that would indicate activities that were conditions for community: membership, personal expression and connection. Parks argued that if an SNS demonstrates all three affordances, then it can be said to be supporting a virtual community. Using MySpace as a case study, Parks examined how often people logged in, how often they updated their profiles and how many friends they were connected to.

Parks' results were surprising. Instead of finding that communities thrived in MySpace, he found that many people (as many as 40 per cent) had so few online friends and logged in so infrequently that it was questionable whether they could even be considered ongoing subscribers to the service, let alone members of any virtual community. Other studies tend to confirm Parks' observations in other social media, although there is also the possibility that the way people use MySpace may differ from the way they use other SNSs like Facebook (Hampton et al. 2011). Only 15 to 25 per cent of surveyed members met Parks' basic requirements for constructing online communities.

Parks also noted, however, that for people with large numbers of friends on MySpace, a high percentage of those friends lived within a relatively small geographical distance from the user. In other words, the online social networks were being used by these people to maintain or supplement existing offline connections. He also suggested that users who find their that friends are already online might be more likely to stay online themselves, and to build communities. The key point here is that these online communities are tightly tied to local relationships, and that offline and online communities are tightly linked – much more so than we might imagine. The Pew Research

Center's Internet & American Life SNS survey conducted in 2010 supports this claim. In this study (which was conducted by phone) it was reported that 89 per cent of North American users' Facebook friends are people they have met more than once in person, and a high percentage of the total number of friends on Facebook are people who are known to the user through school/university, work, family or volunteer groups (Hampton et al. 2011).

This data suggests that SNS relationships are geographically and socially oriented towards the local. Significantly, these findings suggest an important point: it's not just the size of the network that matters, but the quality of the connections. More intimate connections seem to be more valuable and more common for SNS users than large numbers of less intimate connections. This weakens the importance of network effects and increases the relative importance of intimacy, suggesting that rather than being characterised as networked publics, SNS-constructed publics might alternatively be defined as 'intimate publics'.

Intimate publics

The idea behind intimate publics is that as social and mobile media become more pervasive, different modes of using these media mean that increasingly publics are defined by the strength of their relationships, rather than the total number of network connections. The term 'intimacy' when used here not only refers to the common-usage kinds of intimacies that exist between lovers, family members or close friends (though these can and do play a role), but also to intimacies that can exist at a social or cultural level. As Michael Herzfeld observes, cultural intimacy describes the 'social poetics' of the nation-state; it is 'the recognition of those aspects of a cultural identity that are considered a source of external embarrassment but that nevertheless provide insiders with their assurance of common sociality' (1997: 3). To put it a different way, intimacy can be something that exists between strangers because of the common bond they can share by virtue of them belonging to the same cultural group, whether that be a town, city, nation or some other sociological or political grouping. An example might be a small country town where everyone who grew up there knows that the town has a reputation for having the worst weather in the nation (or the most boring night-life, or the most superstitious people in the province and so on). This shared knowledge, even if it is potentially embarrassing, also acts as a kind of social bond – a 'cultural intimacy'.

An example of when cultural intimacies come into play would be when two people from similar cultural backgrounds but who are otherwise strangers accidentally meet on a train in an unfamiliar country, and find that they immediately have a connection. The way that SNSs have been developed or simply picked up by different nations and cultures across the world is also a tangible example of this kind of cultural intimacy. China's QQ is not just any SNS; it is *the* Chinese SNS, and to use QQ is to participate in a community that shares a set of cultural intimacies. Facebook has become popular in Korea, but it does not speak to and of Korea in the way Cyworld minihompy does (Hjorth 2007). One of the first SNSs, Friendster, began in the US but soon became widely adopted in the Philippines. Many Brazilians use Google's original SNS, Orkut. The list of SNSs which have become associated with particular nationalities goes on. In these examples it can be argued that a sense of community emerges through the performance of personal intimacies and the aggregation and identification of public socio-cultural intimacies.

At a more interpersonal level, SNS can be regarded as a technological tool that mediates interpersonal intimacies. Esther Milne (2004) has suggested that new media, such as SNSs, function socially as tools to mediate intimacy, and should be historically contextualised with other technologies that have filled this role. Far from being a new phenomenon, others have argued that intimacy has always been mediated (Hjorth 2005), with examples of other technological intimacy mediators including texting on mobile phones, the telegraph (see, for example, Standage 1998), and written correspondence. When seen in this light, the only thing that has changed with the arrival of SNSs is that people have appropriated computer networks as yet another technology that mediates intimacy.

Intimacy in SNSs is also represented by how people manage their online details. All SNSs have a concept of a profile, or something similar, which reveals something about the user. This profile, as we mentioned above, may include images and other information, and can often be made public or private through the software, with these two categories defined fairly rigidly: sharing with everybody (public) or sharing with friends (private). Google+ introduced the idea of 'circles' that allow people to place friends into different and potentially overlapping user-defined categories like 'work mates' or 'school friends'. The amount of information about oneself that is revealed through the profile is part of the performance of intimacy online.

For boyd (2011), US youth have responded to the growth in networked media by creating networked publics that engage in various forms of semi-public and semi-private modalities. Choosing what to share and who to share it with allows people to control the privacy or publicness of their information that goes beyond the relatively clumsy tools provided by social networks. Instead, people use new kinds of strategies to control their information, carefully assessing the social value of revealing information against the potential costs (boyd and Marwick 2011). Privacy, in other words, is not simply an on/off switch or a setting that is chosen and then ignored. Rather, the boundaries between public and private are something that people are constantly revising as a perpetual work in progress (Hjorth and Arnold 2013). Rather than viewing all SNSs as 'networked publics', as boyd does for the context of the West, we could characterise SNSs instead as 'intimate publics' that are played out, and through, social media practices. Some of these practices are expanded and examined in a Korean context in Chapter 7.

TRENDS IN SNS STUDY

The different perspectives presented above demonstrate that SNS are highly complex phenomena, and virtually demand the social scholar's attention. Reflecting this, the study of SNSs has become prominent within internet studies and related disciplines. One glance at the programme of key annual conferences such as AoIR (Association of Internet Researchers) shows the various methods and approaches in the multitude of papers addressing SNSs. This is hardly surprising as SNSs are highly visible internet phenomena, not only because they are so widely used, but also because they provide a potential wealth of information for researchers about how people interact. Through the popularity of Web 2.0, the riches that have become associated with social media entrepreneurs like Mark Zuckerberg and the corresponding media coverage SNSs have become the 'new new thing' (Lewis 2000).

Much of the research into SNSs until recently has been preoccupied with the uses of SNSs by young people in Western contexts (Goggin and McLelland 2009). However, to think of SNSs as a Western Anglophonic phenomenon would be a mistake, as SNSs are fast becoming a global phenomenon and are no less emergent in developing countries (boyd and Ellison 2007). Surveys of SNS users continually put a lie to the idea that SNSs are the domain of the young. While younger users are often more active on social networks, they are not the dominant age group. For example, the average Facebook user was 38 in 2010 and the average age is increasing every year (Hampton et al. 2011). As the demographic continues to widen, SNSs are also becoming increasingly important sites for emerging forms of familial interaction, socialising, relationship management and identity construction (Bennett 2008; Bennett et al. 2009; Ito et al. 2008; Rheingold 2008; Hjorth and Arnold 2012; Madianou and Miller 2012).

Methodological approaches to the study of social networks also vary. Following on from the virtual ethnographic research traditions we mentioned above (Hine 1998; Miller and Slater 2001), some researchers of SNSs have used qualitative approaches (boyd 2004, 2009, 2011; Miller 2011) to focus upon more detailed, local and personalised understandings of the intimate and social dimensions of SNS use. Other approaches are broader, analysing and criticising social media, or particular aspects of it (Shirky 2008). Studies around SNSs as part of broader forms of twenty-first century media literacy (Ito et al. 2008) have also begun to emerge.

SNSs are also implicated in other areas of research, like journalism, politics and law. As we will see in Chapter 4, social media are enabling changes in the way people engage with politics via citizen journalism and online activism, and SNSs are often the sites and technologies that support these activities. The discussion is thus rapidly moving beyond Western and teen contexts and expanding to engage with broader social issues that include censorship, privacy and copyright. This means that study into SNSs is highly multi-disciplinary, and thus methodologies and motives for research are highly varied. In the remainder of this chapter we are going to paint an impression with broad brush-strokes of some of the major areas of current research that engages with SNSs. As we will see, SNS studies are maturing and multiplying, reflecting the way that SNSs are occupying an increasingly important role both within and across societies.

Non-Anglocentric studies

Initial research into SNSs focused upon contexts familiar with the researcher's own cultural context. Given the nature of English as the *lingua franca* in 'global' studies, many studies into SNSs came from Anglophonic researchers (Goggin and McLelland 2009). Later, non-Anglophonic models began to grow, relating the cross-cultural and global nature of SNSs (Yang et al. 2003; Goggin and McLelland 2009).

This shift is important when we consider that many of the locations for hardware and software manufacturing have been situated in non-Anglophonic contexts. The Asia-Pacific region, which encompasses locations such as India and China, is one such non-Anglophonic context that is home to some of the oldest SNSs such as Cyworld (Hjorth and Kim 2005). Many nations within the Asia-Pacific also have longer histories with mobile and locative technologies (see Chapter 7) and demonstrate examples of new social uses of the technologies in areas such as gaming, location-aware social media and social networks (Hjorth and Chan 2009). This makes the region difficult for researchers to ignore.

Studies of social media use in the Asia-Pacific region, for example, have found that for youth, SNSs are not only a fundamental part of everyday life and the exercise of their social capital (see below), but also a space that helps to maintain intergenerational ties when geographic distance might be involved – a point we will illustrate more clearly through a case study of social media games in Chapter 6.

As studies in the US have found, in many countries in the Asia-Pacific it is no longer just 'youth' that are using SNSs, as adult-to-adult and inter-generational forms of dialogue and digital literacy expand with increased net accessibility. Moreover, the demographics are shifting too, as internet access becomes a tool not just for the rich or middle classes, but as an integral part of a new mobile working class (Qiu 2008). Interestingly, in China it is working-class use of the internet that is growing exponentially, mainly through mobile media (CNNIC 2009). This gives us insight into the ways that some of the largest societies on Earth are developing and integrating new media into this development.

Cross-cultural approaches to the study of SNSs also provide us with insights into the differences and similarities between new media practices in different cultures. By moving the cultural frame to another context, we often find we learn a lot about the way that social media works in our own culture, as behaviours which are rendered invisible through familiarity become visible in unfamiliar cultural contexts.

SNSs and political action

In Chapter 4 we will look at the participative qualities of social media, and the way that political engagement can emerge from activities like citizen journalism and online activism. We will also suggest that mobile technology is playing an increasingly important role in the way that groups of people can organise, as outlined by Howard Rheingold's concept of 'smart mobs' (2002). The possibilities of using SNSs and social media for political action has been further promoted by events, such as the Arab Spring uprisings of 2011, which helped to establish the idea that social media was no longer only about social networks for maintaining interpersonal relationships. Social media was presented here as a powerful communication technology that changed the nature of how information gets disseminated through new affective channels that have the potential to motivate and mobilise people in ways that media has never before – as we will see with the *Kony 2012* campaign example in Chapter 4.

While we need to be cautious about claims that any new technology is very different or revolutionary, in this case this technology is a particularly useful tool for organising and communicating. This is partially because there is a greater degree of affective personalisation involved with social media.

In other words, if you receive a pamphlet about a protest from a stranger in the street it is a different experience to receiving the same information from a friend on Facebook. In the latter example, there's already a connection between you and the friend, so the message has more significance and it is likely to affect you on a different level. Messages can also take on unique forms not just in terms of media format (text, image, video) but also discussion and active engagement through messaging, online petitions and so on (Bennett 2008; Bennett et al. 2009; Ito et al. 2008; Rheingold 2008). Social mobile media also provide new spaces for networked, *effective* civic responses and *affective* interpersonal responses (Hjorth and Arnold 2012).

Privacy

One of the more significant and complex concerns associated with social network sites is the issue of privacy and, not surprisingly, this is a burgeoning area in the field of SNS research. This issue has received a great deal of attention not just in popular media, but in critical literature as well. Privacy is a highly popular topic precisely because it is so complex, and because it provides a handhold for anchoring fears and anxieties about a new technology.

Most new technologies are met with an initial social response that contains elements of fear, paranoia and anxiety (Kember 1998). The media frequently plays into these fears, often emphasising them out of proportion by focusing on the exceptional and presenting it as the norm. SNSs are no exception to this, and have been implicated as the culprits in a range of modern anxieties from playground bullying to terrorism. The media is happy to offer a range of anecdotes to support these fears (Marwick 2008).

For SNSs, concerns about privacy are tantamount. Parents worry that their children are able to publish too much about themselves, attracting unwanted attention, damaging their reputations or breaking laws that they may not even realise they are breaking. For their part, teenagers often resent their parents' interest in their online activities, and see parental attempts at monitoring their online behaviour as an invasion of their privacy (boyd and Marwick 2011).

Some studies have examined the uses of SNSs and their built-in privacy systems and have concluded that many users of SNSs – especially younger users – do not take advantage of the privacy features (Gross and Acquisti 2005). Others suggest that to understand young people's attitudes to privacy in the online environment requires a more thorough understanding of online practices. boyd and Hargittai (2010), for example, show that teens in their studies are very aware of the privacy implications of their online activities and are very selective about what they share and who they share it with.

Much of the work on privacy concerns the relationship between individuals and how people negotiate, public and private, between themselves and other users of the SNS. However, another dimension of privacy that has been less explored concerns the relationship between users and the SNS itself. The issues associated with this go back to fundamental questions about user and used, and control, that we examined in Chapter 2.

Analysing social data

As we saw in Chapter 2, SNSs collect and generate data about their users and about how users connect with each other. Although much of the data that SNSs collect remains private, some of that data is public, especially those things that the users themselves want to share. An example is posts on Twitter, which provide information such as time and date sent, sometimes a geographic location for the originating post, the user name of the person who created the post and so on. The richness of Twitter posts also comes from the use of hashtags, which allow people to track issues rather than individuals.

Many SNSs now provide application programmable interfaces (APIs) that allow various applications, including custom-built applications, to access the data generated by the SNS. This can provide researchers with a wealth of information about the use of the SNS, but can also provide enticing glimpses into the social machinery. Research using this data has resulted in a wide range of different applications. For example, Bamman et al. (2012) have used statistical analysis techniques on data from Twitter and Sina Weibo (a Chinese SNS, similar to Twitter) and Chinese instant messaging services to gain an understanding of levels and application of censorship in mainland China. From their analysis they claimed to be able to identify terms that were censored and even to show how censorship varied by province.

Data visualisation techniques are increasingly being used to provide visual representations of the data, too. In this work, large amounts of data collected from an SNS is used to draw images, charts and graphs which reflect some aspect of the SNS. For example, Facebook intern Paul Butler (2010) used data on the location and frequency of Facebook posts, resulting in a map that lights up the world based on Facebook use. Large chunks of Africa, China and Russia are rendered dark, providing a startling visual mapping of population density, global wealth and aggressive censorship.

In a similar vein, Jer Thorp, a Canadian artist and educator, developed *Just Landed In …*, a visualisation of the location of Twitter posts that contain the phrase 'just landed in'. In this visualisation, lines appear superimposed across the globe, representing people's travel and providing a visual representation of human movement through space and time and their connections with social media (Thorp 2009).

Others are using social media sources and applying sophisticated information processing techniques to explore the relationships and uses of SNSs as a way of providing quantitative data that supports (or refutes) qualitative research. Thelwall has conducted a number of such analyses of SNSs. In one such study, Thelwall (2008) collected a random selection of around 20,000 profiles from MySpace users and analysed the information provided in these profiles to develop a statistical overview of data such as age, religion, frequency of access and so on. Thelwall found that users were younger than previously reported (the median age was 21), and that the median number of friends was 27. He also saw that there were groupings of this data; there were a lot of people who only had 1 friend, a group who had 2–9 friends, another that had 10–90 and a third group who had more than 90. The authors noted that this was consistent with qualitative research that suggested that people who use MySpace categorise friends into close friends, acquaintances and strangers. Given that the median was 27 friends, the data suggested that for MySpace users, most friends were acquaintances rather than close friends. The suggestion here is that people made friends online, rather than using the SNS as a way to maintain offline relationships. This is at odds with some research, although it may also reflect the kinds of users that were using MySpace.

Others still are using social media data to gain insights into how people respond to events. For one example, Bruns et al. (2012) analysed social media postings in the aftermath of the 2011 floods in Brisbane, Australia. They followed the changing social media etiquette and the response by the Queensland police to the disaster through large-scale data collection of Twitter hashtags, and then created visualisations of the patterns of media use and themes around this event. For another example, in Hjorth and Kim's (2011) case study of the role of social and mobile media in the crisis of Japan's earthquake, tsunami and Fukushima nuclear reactor disaster (known as 3/11), they found that many victims of these events relied on older media and communication methods. This seemed to be because the participatory nature of social media made understanding the event more confusing than when it was encountered through 'packaged' media like television. One respondent noted that prior to 3/11 he had viewed Twitter as 'conversational', but during and after the crisis his opinion changed dramatically; he felt bombarded by conflicting social media threads which then made him redefine the discourse surrounding Twitter as more like a 'conference' than a 'conversation'.

If we are to understand the impact of social media in times of crisis or political upheaval we need to move our analysis from an *effect*-orientated focus to *affect*-orientated one. We need more hybrid studies that combine the micro and macro analysis, using such methods as Ken Anderson's 'ethno-mining' in which ethnographic processes are used to analyse data-mining (Anderson et al. 2009). Data-mining and visualisations may paint pictures of media phenomenon during these times, but as anyone who has lost an intimate will attest, they are abstract in the reality of grief's texture. Instead, there needs to be more ethnographies of media affect and mobile intimacy to understand the micro, meso and macro levels of intimate publics in times of trauma.

There is certainly a proliferation of data in current society, leading some to call this moment the 'era of Big Data'. However, as boyd and Crawford note, 'Big Data' is 'in many ways, a poor term' (2012: 663). They argue that:

> like other socio-technical phenomena, Big Data triggers both utopian and dystopian rhetoric. On one hand, Big Data is seen as a powerful tool to address various societal ills, offering the potential of new insights into areas as diverse as cancer research, terrorism, and climate change. On the other, Big Data is seen as a troubling manifestation of Big Brother, enabling invasions of privacy, decreased civil freedoms, and increased state and corporate control. As with all socio-technical phenomena, the currents of hope and fear often obscure the more nuanced and subtle shifts that are under way. (2012: 663–4)

Representations of Big Data are compelling, illustrating Matt Jones' point that data is seductive material (2009). Data holds the promise of containing answers to questions you haven't even asked yet, so long as you have the tools to collect, sort and analyse the dataset. But this can be a compelling illusion, as there are limits to what the data alone can tell us, especially when it comes to the analysis of social data. Sentiment analysis, for example, is a technique where the computer attempts to determine the affective meaning pieces of text. This is done through statistical analysis of words and word proximity. So, a piece of text like 'I'm having the worst day of my life' could be analysed and determined to be a negative sentiment. However, the computer cannot read context. When one person claims that a particular person is 'sick', for example, it has different meanings that depend on the person being referred to and the person doing the referring. Kamvar and Harris's

We Feel Fine (2009), which builds up an interactive mapping on sentiment in blog posts, is probably still the most engaging use of sentiment analysis even though their purpose is more artistic than analytical. As Anderson et al. (2009) note, data mining by itself provides little insight beyond abstract pattern recognition. Forwarding their hybrid model of 'ethno-mining', Anderson et al. argue that the socio-cultural depth provided by ethnography needs to be brought to data mining in order to render these abstractions into dynamic reflections of lives and subjectivities.

The use of data analysis techniques as a research tool raises a number of issues. boyd and Crawford (2011, 2012) point to a number of them, including issues with the ethics of using public data that was never intended to be used in this fashion, the methodological reliability and limits to the approaches used (sentiment analysis is an obvious problem here) and the potential of uneven and inequitable access to data sources. As boyd and Crawford observe, the 'Big Data' move should be understood as part of the *computational turn* (Burkholder 1992) that, in turn, creates new digital divides. This is an emerging and valuable area of research in social media that would benefit from a more rigorous examination of its techniques.

CONCLUSION

In many ways, SNSs are *the* definitive social media technology. They are the interface through which people engage with social media, and increasingly they are the way that people engage with the internet. SNSs are shining examples of the Web 2.0 ethos we discussed in Chapter 2 – they are user-oriented, providing a space for people to make things, share things, communicate and connect with each other, allowing for a wide range of empowering practices from activism to creative production. However, we must not forget that they are also commercial ventures, and as such can and do commercialise users by collecting and using their data and details. SNSs are free, in that we do not pay subscription fees to access them, but companies like Facebook have multi-billion dollar valuations. The question we must ask here is, why? If we are not paying in cash then are we paying in some other way, and are we getting value?

In the first part of this chapter we have looked at the evolution of the internet as a medium for sociality. From virtual communities we have explored networks, networked publics and intimacy as structural features of the sociality afforded by SNSs. Questions persist about whether SNSs and online interactions are better understood as a network or a community. We suggest that SNSs exhibit properties of both.

SNSs are also both global and local. From Manchester to Manila, and from Seoul to Sydney, people are using SNSs for similar reasons, and in this way they are a powerful symbol of the way that communication technologies really are spanning the globe, crossing cultures and encouraging research that appreciates the diversity this represents. Yet SNSs are also intensely local, emphasising rather than erasing geographical proximity. SNSs may span the globe, but the relationships we maintain through them are generally those that we also maintain through face-to-face contact.

There is, of course, a faddish element to SNSs, and it is likely that today's darlings of the digerati will be tomorrow's old news, but it would be a mistake to dismiss SNSs as nothing more than a fashion, as they reflect social practice as much as they create it. SNSs have not become popular because they create social networks, but because they provide a space for social networks to exist. These social networks, as we have seen throughout this chapter, and indeed in other chapters, exist in both online and offline worlds. They provide spaces for online relations, but also structure our offline relationships.

4 Participation and user created content

If there is one word that summarises the particular quality of social media, it would be 'participation'. Unlike the mass media before it, social media is fundamentally a participative medium. Our online experience increasingly involves methods of actively providing information about what we are doing, or what we think of something. This might be as simple as a Facebook 'like' button, or as involved as maintaining a blog. Participation can take various forms of agency from user generated content (UGC), in which users forward content made by others, to user created content (UCC), in which the content is made by the user. Every time we participate we partake in various forms of labour sharing – from creative and social to emotional and affective labour. In each cultural context, what it means to participate takes on different dimensions. For example, in China where the internet is highly regulated by the government, participation can often take the form of what in the West might be called 'lurking'. After all, imagine if the 457 million internet users (CIW 2012) all spoke online at once. If everyone were talking, who would be listening? Indeed, listening as a form of participation has only recently gained attention in critical work concerning social media (Crawford 2009).

The emergence of social media and its emphasis on participative modes of use has many significant implications for the study of media and society more broadly. In each location, the implications of 'click-activism' are playing out with different results (Nugroho and Syarief 2012). For example, we can see changes in the fabric of activism in the emergence of social uprisings like the Occupy Wall Street movement, or the Arab Spring uprisings of 2011 (Diamond and Plattner 2012). New dimensions are added to crisis management and response as seen during the New Zealand earthquake of 2011 (Bruns et al. 2012) and the events of Japan's 3/11 tsunami (Hjorth and Kim 2011). Perhaps most significantly for journalists, social media is throwing up challenges to the privileged position of journalists and the news media as the sole arbiters of reportage. As participative forms of media like blogs and SNSs become more mainstream, we are seeing the rise of the citizen journalist – a phenomenon that is challenging conventions around press media and journalism in general (Meikle and Redden 2010). It is important not to grant social media too much agency when examining its role in political events: social media didn't cause these events, but it did change the context for distribution and participation. In short, we are witnessing a shift in the *affect*, rather than *effect*, and this has effects on other spheres of society such as political agency and online activism.

The impact of the participative features of social media has been studied by a number of scholars from a number of different perspectives. Bruns et al. (2012) found that the use of social media, Facebook and Twitter played an important role in crisis communication at the height of the 2011 South-East Queensland floods crisis. In their report they focused upon the role of Twitter 'in disseminating and sharing crisis information and updates from state and local authorities as well as everyday citizens' (Bruns et al. 2012: 7). In his discussion of the political capacities of political fans and Twitter faking, Jason Wilson argues that such mobile and social media 'are interwoven with emerging, fan-like forms of engagement with mediatised politics' (2011: 1). In what he calls 'post-broadcast democracies', activities such as Twitter 'faking' show 'playful, performative and mobile dimensions, which challenge scholars to rethink theories of play, performance, fandom and political engagement' (Wilson 2011: 1). Hjorth and Kim's analysis of social media for crisis management in the wake of Japan's 3/11 asks whether we can think about a social and mobile media 'affect' in the ways in which it frames people's responses. They argue that 'while social media provide new channels for affective cultures in the form of mobile intimacy, they also extend on earlier media practices and rituals such as the postcard' (Hjorth and Kim 2011: 1).

Central to these discussions about the politics of social and mobile media is a rethinking of the relationship between participation, agency and media. In this light, it is important to recognise that media 'participation' is a culturally specific notion. Let us return to the opening example of China. While 'lurking' in an Anglophonic context evokes images of users being passive (Crawford 2009), in China such an activity is seen as an important part of media participation (Goggin and Hjorth 2009). As social and mobile media evolve unevenly across the globe, we see the ways in which that media reflects local cultural, social and economic nuances. By engaging with a culturally divergent understanding of participation that complicates the binary between empowerment and exploitation, we reflect upon the evolution of 'participatory media' (Jenkins 2006) and how this has shaped, and been shaped by, social media (Bennett 2008; Rheingold 2008). In order to explore what participation means, and how it has been theorised and represented in the social media literature, we will investigate a few broad areas of academic study.

First, we will expand upon one of the threads explored in Chapter 2 and engage more deeply with how academic scholars have conceptualised the idea of audiences/users as producers. We also deploy Bruns' term 'produser', which we think is a very helpful term for describing the kinds of productive behaviours to be addressed in this chapter. After we have defined what we mean by produser, we will tackle another slightly more straightforward and related theme: user created content (UCC). We will define what we mean by these terms, contextualise them within the literature and then go on to look at some of the implications of produsage and UCC.

Once we have defined the ideas of users as co-producers and of UCC, we will move on to look at how these concepts play out in more generalised and grounded practice. First, we will consider crowd sourcing as one way that combined user production can be utilised to great effect in an online environment filled with literally millions of users. We will then examine the phenomenon of citizen journalism, before going on to examine online activism, both quite practical examples of the kinds of behaviours that participatory media enable. We will limit our discussion of journalism in light of the book's focus upon social media. Entire books have been written about citizen journalism (Gillmor 2006; Meikle and Redden 2010) and online activism (Zuckerman 2008; Pickerill 2010; Lovink 2012), and where relevant, we encourage you to refer to these works if you want to develop a more thorough understanding of the phenomena.

USERS AS PRODUCERS – 'PRODUSERS'

As we saw in Chapter 2, the premise of Web 2.0 and the associated shift in audiences has become a kind of reaction to the growing understanding that in networked communication environments the audience are no longer simply consumers of media: they have become participants. Just what participation means in the context of online media is very fuzzy indeed. In general terms, we can say that internet-based media is participative because it is two-way. This phenomenon has led some people to describe certain kinds of uses of the internet as participative or participatory media (Rheingold 2008). One aspect of participation is public response. Commenting on a news story in an online newspaper is a kind of participation, although it is a kind of participation that rehearses earlier types of media such as radio talkback and letters to the editor of a newspaper. This kind of participation is something that has been written about widely, especially in social media and Web-2.0-branded marketing texts. The common exhortation you will see repeated by marketers is that the web is a conversation, a rhetoric that has become a contemporary business mantra.

A much more provocative idea, however, is the idea of the audience as media producer. This takes the idea of participation to another level. Instead of simply responding to content that has been created by an organisation, here the user becomes the source of the original material. Bloggers become journalists, fans become the authors of extensions to books and films (Jenkins 1992, 2006). Your kid becomes a star on YouTube because millions of people think he was funny after he had visited the dentist and was still zonked out on anaesthetic.[1] If you have ever watched a funny video on YouTube or been sent an email containing a funny picture, then the chances are very high that the material was produced by another user – a person a bit like you who was armed with nothing more than their laptop or desktop computer, some technical skill and a clever idea. This kind of participation, which is made possible by internet media (and exploited by social media), tells us that the internet user is perhaps not best characterised as a member of an audience, with its associated implications of passivity. This kind of user – the person who makes videos, songs, sounds, images and writings and shares them online – is something more active, something that looks more like a producer.

In terms of scholarly approaches to the idea of user production of media, there have been a number of papers and books written by some well-respected and influential academics. One of the first to stake a claim in this territory was Henry Jenkins, whose earlier work closely explored fan communities in which he persuasively argued that fans were producers (1992). As a cultural theorist, Jenkins comes from a tradition of cultural media research that is interested in how audiences use and make meaning from the media. Stuart Hall's seminal work *Encoding and Decoding in the Television Discourse* (1973) argued that television audiences are not passive but active consumers of the media. They are active in that they construct their own meanings from media 'texts' that may not be entirely in line with the intended meaning of the producers.

Jenkins' early work in this area, which pre-dates the development of the internet as a mainstream medium, looked at fan cultures. He was particularly interested in the way that fans of TV series like *Star Trek*, for example, did not simply watch the show, but actively engaged with it through a series of highly visible creative practices which include everything from making outfits and role-playing characters at conventions to extending plots and the storyworld of the show by writing fictional narratives of their own. The film *Trekkies* (directed by Roger Nygard, 1997), in which *Star Trek* fans are divided into two types – Trekkies and Trekkers – is a good example of different levels of 'fandom' participation. Trekkers might be fans in that they watch the show and buy some merchandise, while Trekkies actively render their lives into characters and storyworlds of *Star Trek*. In other words, Trekkers might visit *Star Trek* whereas Trekkies completely inhabit the world of *Star Trek*. Thus, engagement with the TV series was much more than passive watching; it was highly creative and active with audiences participating in the making of meanings and interpretations. Indeed, it was in these fan communities – both those of gamers (we will come back to this in Chapter 5) and fans of popular culture – that the first kinds of production emerged, well before anyone coined the term 'Web 2.0', and well before the first social media sites appeared. In reflecting on these observations, Jenkins describes something he called a 'participatory culture', which he defines as:

> a culture with relatively low barriers to artistic expression and civic engagement, strong support for creating and sharing one's creations, and some type of informal mentorship whereby what is known by the most experienced is passed along to novices. A participatory culture is also one in which members believe their contributions matter, and feel some degree of social connection with one another (at the least they care what other people think about what they have created). (2006: 3)

While Jenkins was concerned with the way that audiences produced, others pointed to the emergence of a new class of worker – the professional amateur, or 'pro-am' – whose production did not fit into ideas of either amateur production or professional production, but occupied a territory somewhere between (Leadbeater et al. 2004). The professional amateur was someone who worked at their interest like a professional, spending as many hours on their endeavour as they might in their day job, treating it like it was a task that earned money, and yet was not a professional since they were not part of a professional community and did not get paid for their work.

Other scholars looked more intently at the way in which users who produced undertook their work. Australian academic Bruns has engaged with the idea of the user who produces through his book *Blogs, Wikipedia, Second Life and Beyond* (2008), in which he describes the term 'produser' as a conflation of the words producer and user. This coining of a new phrase is not just about coming up with a word to mark academic territory; it is also about developing a word that is simply lacking in the English language to describe something that has become so ubiquitous that it is simpler to use a new word than to continue using a phrase.

Other terms have also been coined, but as yet none have stuck. The idea and practices are quite new, and it will be some time before the phrases are resolved. Perhaps in the future we may simply return to a term like 'user', and simply incorporate the understanding that users are also producers into this term. In any event, the term 'produser' is useful in the context of this discussion, and you will find that throughout this book we use Bruns' term when we are referring to users who produce.

USER CREATED CONTENT (UCC)

There is a wealth of information online, and a great deal of it is produced by users working in their own free time. Creating content not only involves creativity but also time, emotion and various forms of capital (social, cultural and sometimes economic). With the availability of high-quality cameras connected to smartphones, the ways in which we can record, experience, visualise and memorialise events is changing (Ito and Okabe 2005, 2006; Hjorth 2007; Mørk Petersen 2008). Many social media sites including YouTube, Flickr and Facebook, to name only a few, exist only because of the content created by their users (Burgess 2007; Mørk Petersen 2008). These sites – more services or 'platforms' than places that actually produce content – make money by selling attention, and that attention is gained through users' creative and social labour. An active part of the media discourses involve forwarding content to other users – often generically called 'user generated content' (UGC).

Not all of this information is produced directly with the implicit intention of making something for someone else to enjoy. Recorded conversations between users is one example. A vast majority of conversations may be of absolutely no interest to other people. Many of these micronarrative gestures seek to reinforce existing relationships and social capital (Ellison et al. 2011). A conversation on Facebook between two friends about what they did on the weekend plays an important role in building and maintaining offline relationships in the online space, but is unlikely to have a great deal of value to others outside this relationship. But this does not mean that all online conversations have little value. For example, a conversation between a few people about their cats' health problems that leads to a resolution might have a great deal of interest for other cat owners who find themselves in the unhappy position of having a sick feline friend. Other information that comes under the overall heading of UGC includes information that users supply about themselves on personal profiles, such as birthdate, gender, physical location and so on. This information may be even less interesting to the average user, but as we discussed in Chapter 3, it is of great value to the SNS that collects it for data-mining.

While all of this material is clearly created by users, and it can become content that is useful to other people, there is a difference between user profile data and a carefully crafted blog post that is uploaded to the internet for the express purpose of being read by other users, or a short film that may represent many hours of production work that is then uploaded to YouTube. In this book we draw a distinction between content that has been created purposefully by a user expressly for exhibition to others, and content that is generated by users as a result of using social media. We use the term 'UCC' to more precisely refer to the kinds of content produced intentionally by users, usually for the purpose of consumption by other users.

There have been a number of criticisms of UCC, some of which we explore in more detail in other chapters (see Chapter 5, for example). One of these criticisms is that (often) amateur UCC is displacing established forms of content creation where the content creator is a professional who has significant training and experience in their field. This is a pronounced criticism in some fields, such as journalism and the arts, as we will see below. In seeking to move the discussion of user creativity beyond the professional/amateur dichotomy, Jean Burgess (2007) has used the term 'vernacular creativity' to identify UCC as something that is characterised by the vernacular and everyday. She points out that while creativity is often seen as the exclusive domain of trained elites like artists or design professionals, creativity has always been an activity that everybody engages in, even if in the past it was not always visible.

Scrapbooking, writing of short stories, and family histories, home crafts and decoration are all examples of vernacular creativity that are no less creative just because they are not produced by professionals or widely accessible in the public domain. For Burgess these activities are about cultural citizenship, a concept that expands and redefines classical notions of citizenship that are based on participation in political activity. Here, the production of creative works acts as a way of asserting and defining one's citizenship, which is 'practised as much through everyday life, leisure, critical consumption and popular entertainment as it is through debate and engagement with capital "P" politics' (Burgess et al. 2006: 1). We will return to some of these issues around UCC in Chapter 5 when we come to look at art and cultural production in the age of social media.

CROWD SOURCING, SMART MOBS, WIKIPEDIA

A person is smart. People are dumb, panicky dangerous animals and you know it. (*Men in Black,* dir. Sonnenfeld 1997)

[U]nder the right circumstances, groups are remarkably intelligent, and are often smarter than the smartest people in them. (Surowiecki 2004: xiii)

While some of the material about user participation explores cases where individual produsers can participate in activities that were once beyond them, others focus on the action of groups of users working together to produce materials or solve problems. James Surowiecki's *Wisdom of Crowds* (2004) explored the idea that large groups of people can often solve problems that individuals within the crowd cannot. Tim O'Reilly picked up this idea and worked it into his formulation of Web 2.0 (2005).

Extrapolating from this idea, Amazon launched their Mechanical Turk service in 2005, which allowed people to either pay a fee to have some problem worked on by a group, or on the flip-side, to be paid a small fee for participation in helping to solve a larger problem. Other online services provide facilities that allow users to associate tags (single words or short phrases) with content, thus allowing large numbers of people to build up keyword indexes based on human-entered information.

The National Library of Australia has also utilised crowd sourcing to help fix text from scanned newspapers for their online Trove service. Trove is a digital repository of Australian media, including print, images and audio. Part of their archive consists of newspapers dating back to 1803, resulting in millions of pages of newsprint available online. These pages were passed through an optical character recognition (OCR) process that automatically turned the printed text into electronic text, which allows the text to be indexed and searched. This is clearly a very valuable resource for historians. However, OCR is not perfect and newsprint – especially material that is smudged or damaged – does not always scan correctly. To fix this a person needs to read the original text, compare it to the OCR text and make any corrections manually. For a collection the size of Trove, this is an intimidating amount of work.

In order to tackle the sheer size of this task, the National Library of Australia developed an interface that allowed anyone on the internet to register and edit the text themselves. This has proved a very successful way of using crowd-sourcing techniques to help produce a publicly accessible, searchable archive. The success can be measured in part by metrics. An early version of the service was released in July 2008 and as of February 2009, 2.2 million lines and 104,000 articles had been corrected by internet users (Holley 2009). While this is only a small percentage of the total 3.5 million articles in Trove (which is planned to increase to 40 million), the strong engagement of the community so rapidly suggests that there is a great deal of value in crowd-sourced applications, especially when people perceive they are helping the community. As one person noted about her motivation for fixing material on Trove:

'I enjoy the correction – it's a great way to learn more about past history and things of interest whilst doing a "service to the community" by correcting text for the benefit of others' but also, her motivation for continuing to change pages was driven by 'the knowledge that you are doing something that will benefit future people that wish to access articles on their family history'. (Holley 2009: 17)

This gives us a small insight into the kinds of motivations that drive user participation. If Mechanical Turk and the Trove experience demonstrate the power of crowds, then Wikipedia provides a compelling case for the power of utilising millions of online users to create an online knowledge repository. Wikipedia is a portmanteau of two words – 'wiki' and 'encyclopaedia'. The word 'wiki' was developed from a Hawaiian word that means 'quick'. In practical terms, a wiki is a web-based system, developed by Ward Cunningham in 1994, that allows people to write and edit a shared document, which can be quickly linked to other documents. This allows a group of people to collaborate on the production of documents that contain a hierarchical and inter-linked arrangement of content. A perfect use for this kind of service is the production of documents that consist of small chunks of self-contained information that have relationships with other chunks of information – a user manual for a piece of software, a technical manual for a mechanical device, or an encyclopaedia.

Realising this potential, the founders of Wikipedia sought to create the world's largest repository of knowledge on just about any topic imaginable. To facilitate this, they created a wiki that they then opened to everyone to contribute to. Wikipedia has quickly become the world's largest source of knowledge on a variety of topics, from the history of the Roman Empire to biographies of actors who starred in obscure cult TV shows. Anyone can create pages in Wikipedia, and anyone can also edit or amend information on Wikipedia – allowing not only for the creation of a wide variety of information, but also for an iterative process of correction and amendment, towards the goal that over time the quality of the entire source will improve.

Some of the major issues with crowd-sourcing come from a failure to recognise its limitations. The main limitation is the inherent fallibility of crowds and the disproportionate ability of a committed individual or small group to bias results. As soon as the Mechanical Turk services started, for example, people quickly found ways to maximise the amount they could earn by providing random results or by automating their input. This means that certain kinds of activities that might utilise the service are open to abuse. Wikipedia, while offering far more information than traditional encyclopaedias, cannot assert the same level of quality that an encyclopaedia with a tightly controlled editorial process can. While the crowd will tend to correct errors and omissions, individuals and groups who have strong views will attempt to sway articles to reflect their points of view, which has led to some significant disagreements over certain contentious subjects.

CITIZEN JOURNALISM

Citizen journalism is fundamentally about the collision between traditional news reporting and participative media. In the online environment, users can take an active role in the production of content, and when this extends to reporting on events, it constitutes citizen journalism (although as we will see this definition makes the issue seem more clear-cut than it is). Citizen journalism has appeared at the intersection between the challenges faced by traditional news reporting in the internet age, the emergence of social media and the growing ubiquity of devices like mobile phones that can capture images and video. For some like Gerard Goggin, the rise of mobile media such as the camera phone, along with personal but broadcast media like Twitter, has made messages, contexts and content more intimate (2011). As part of a broader movement of intimacy into the public realm (Berlant 1998), the role of mobile media – as one of the most personal and intimate devices (Fortunati 2002) – has had an impact upon journalism. With 'amateur' images taken by the mobile phone having more of a raw and unpolished feel, the texture of visuality in journalism has changed. It is not uncommon for a journalist to evoke that amateur feel to give the news a more intimate and trustworthy affect. The use of camera phones to shift notions of intimacy and place is discussed further in Chapter 7.

In the contemporary media landscape, one of the areas that has come under the most pressure is news reporting, and in particular, newspapers. Newspapers, which have long been supported by advertising revenue, have steadily lost this revenue to the internet as advertisers follow user attention online. Compounding this, many online news sources offer content for free and directly compete with traditional newspapers for their readers. This loss in revenue for newspapers results in increased pressure for newspapers and related news organisations to find cheaper ways to produce and present the news. Social media offers an interesting alternative for the collection of news stories, allowing news organisations to crowd-source content which not only gives them access to content that would not have been possible to get in years past but also to get it for very little money.

So what is citizen journalism?

While the internet has allowed users to write and contribute from its earliest days, it is only since the emergence of social media that the tools for doing this became mainstream. The chief technology associated with citizen journalism has been blogs, which made the publication of material on the internet accessible to people who did not possess the knowledge and skills required to set up and maintain a web server, or organise their own hosting (both of which require a fairly high level of technical knowledge).

Another key feature in the emergence of citizen journalism is the growing ubiquity of mobile media devices – primarily mobile phones – that allow users to take photos and videos, and which are always with millions of people all the time. This means that when an event occurs where there are people to see it, there is frequently also footage, courtesy of someone's ever-handy mobile phone. Following the London bombings in 2005, for example, the BBC received hundreds of videos and thousands of images from the public (Stuart 2007). Furthermore, with the growing uptake of internet-enabled smartphones, content can be both captured and shared within minutes of an event occurring. When linked to social networks like Twitter or Facebook, news can break very quickly and reach an audience much faster than traditional media – especially print media – can respond to. These same features of mobile and social media also have significant implications for online activism, which we will deal with in the following section.

Citizen journalism takes a number of forms, and there is some debate about what does and what does not constitute citizen journalism. There has also been significant criticism of the term, as we will see. Fundamental to all expressions of citizen journalism is the idea that the person doing the reporting is independent and does not work for a media organisation. This leaves a broad range of practices and forums that can be considered citizen journalism. At one end of the spectrum are user comments or feedback on news articles, which allow user participation but maintain the production of news stories within a more traditional editorial setting. These are borderline cases of citizen journalism, as the news organisation maintains tight editorial control over the published story and in many cases also exercises control over the comments posted about the story.

Some sites, like Slashdot and Kuro5hin, for example, feature news stories submitted by users of the site, and encourage commentary on the stories to the point where it is the feedback of the readers (some of which are highly knowledgeable about the topic material) that becomes the most important feature of the sites. Here, the stories act as catalysts for discussion, and a participative moderation system allows readers to rate comments, ideally promoting the more insightful or interesting comments above the banal or poorly thought-out.

There are other sites that are built on a participatory model, where the news reported is sourced almost entirely from users. In Australia, The Conversation is a news site that provides an editorial framework for the publication of stories written by Australian academics. In Korea, OhmyNews has provided a forum since 1999 for anyone to publish news stories under the slogan 'every citizen is a reporter'. Dozens of similar sites exist in countries across the world.

In Australia and the UK, government-supported national broadcasters (the Australian Broadcasting Corporation (ABC) and the British Broadcasting Corporation (BBC)) support sites that draw from the community, and are actively engaged in exploring the possibilities of citizen journalism. ABC's The Drum, for example, is an opinion site that merges commentary from journalists and politicians with submissions from the public. Stories posted to The Drum go through an editorial process, and are presented on the site for public viewing.

At the other end of the spectrum are the blogs or websites that report on news where an individual or small group post messages to report on events. Some of the best-known examples of citizen journalism fall into this category. Salam Abdulmunem (better known by his alias Salam Pax), a blogger based in Iraq, became a well-known figure during the Second Gulf War as he reported on the progress of the war as a local Iraqi from his home in Baghdad. Following the terrorist attacks on the US of September 11, 2001, Glenn Reynolds' blog *Instapundit.com* attracted a large following, pushing Reynolds into fame as another blogger who had the impact and audience normally enjoyed only by professional journalists.

Live tweeting has also become a significant phenomenon in recent years. Here people who are present at a newsworthy event – be it a press conference or perhaps a disaster – use instant messaging tools like Twitter to replay short updates, possibly inflected with personal observations or commentary. This can be very powerful as a form of news as it operates in real time, allowing thousands or millions of people to follow an event as it unfolds, rather than waiting for a regular news briefing or the morning paper. With intimate devices like mobile phones functioning to collect and disseminate events almost immediately, the aforementioned intimate turn in journalism has seen an aestheticisation of this effect for more audience affect. This intimacy makes the content and context of mobile media appear more trustworthy and everyday, although of course this may not be the case as the identity and motivations of the reporter are opaque. This immediacy also has other drawbacks, as we will see below.

There is an overlap between traditional journalism and citizen journalism, with many trained journalists working for news organisations maintaining blogs and other forms of social media to provide a channel for news, inflected with the individual journalists' own perspectives on the issues at hand. Many, like Dan Gillmor, see citizen journalism as being a positive development overall. Gillmor, a journalist with more than 25 years' experience, is highly critical of the rise of what he calls 'Big Media' and the negative effects this has had upon journalism. His 2006 book *We the Media* is probably the best-known text on the topic of citizen journalism. For Gillmor, Big Media are large companies that treat the news as a commodity, where costs of making news are pushed down while profits are maximised, a strategy which Gillmor (amongst others) argues is rarely aligned with good journalism.

In this environment, citizen journalism offers an alternative to mainstream media, filling what Gillmor sees as a middle ground that has been opened as Big Media has shifted its focus to 'light' news which focuses on celebrity gossip and violence (2006: 5). In Australia, for example, the news media is highly concentrated into two companies: Rupert Murdoch's News Limited and John Fairfax Holdings Ltd. In the 2007 Australian federal elections, citizen journalists emerged as an alternative to the mainstream media, and actively criticised the reportage of the Big Media organisations through their blogs. *The Australian* – the only national daily newspaper in Australia that felt threatened enough by this criticism to come out with an article attacking citizen journalists – described them as 'sheltered academics and failed journalists who would not get a job on a real newspaper' (cited in Bruns et al. 2008).

Gillmor sees the evolution of citizen journalism as paralleling a trajectory of increasing user participation in the production of content. He sees this as an evolutionary process 'from journalism as lecture to journalism as a conversation or seminar [which] will force the various communities of interest to adapt' (Gillmor 2006: xxiv). This characterisation of online behaviour as a conversation is a recurring theme in much of the non-academic literature, as we noted in the beginning of this chapter.

Criticisms of citizen journalism

While proponents point to some significant potential for citizen journalism, there are also many criticisms that point to problems and limitations inherent in the form. One criticism, which is often levelled by professional journalists, is that citizen journalists lack the training and rigour of professional journalists. Critics argue that citizen journalists consequently don't have the skills to get stories that trained journalists are able to break, because trained journalists have better access to people and have honed their skills in interviewing and research. In effect, this argues that there is more to journalism than having a publication platform, and that participative media, in providing people with a platform, is not enough to make them journalists. This argument does not necessarily dismiss the value of citizen journalists, but emphasises the need for professionally trained journalists even in an era of participative media.

Another serious criticism of citizen journalism is that it lacks the transparency of traditional news media. Citizen journalists do not need to follow professional codes of conduct. Furthermore, while a professional journalist is kept in check by editorial processes, citizen journalists are free to write whatever they want. Any political affiliations or bias on the part of the citizen journalist is therefore harder to determine, bringing the impartiality and accuracy of their work into question, and placing more responsibility on the reader to determine the quality of the source. Trust becomes a major issue that was in the past mitigated to some degree by the reputation of the news source.

Citizen journalists are also far more vulnerable than journalists working for news organisations because they lack the protection that is often extended to them as employees. Some of the best journalism provokes strong responses from people and opens journalists to legal (and sometimes physical) retaliation. Journalists working for news companies enjoy a certain amount of protection, especially legal protection against civil litigation (for example, being sued for libel). Because citizen journalists are working for themselves they have no overarching protection, which in some circumstances seriously compromises their ability to report on provocative issues. As Dan Gillmor asks:

> Who would have exposed the Watergate crimes in the absence of powerful publishers, especially the *Washington Post*'s Katharine Graham, who had the financial and moral fortitude to stand up to Richard Nixon and his henchmen? (Gillmor 2006: xxvii)

The speed with which social media allows news to be distributed also raises issues. Traditionally, the professional journalist's job was not simply to relay pieces of information to their readers, but to sort rumour from fact, to analyse and synthesise a story from multiple, often-contradictory sources. With instant messaging services like Twitter, news can be disseminated so rapidly that it bypasses normal editorial control, potentially leading to incorrect and misleading reports being released which are then left to readers to analyse and evaluate. The short 140 characters or less format of Twitter in many ways remediates its technological predecessor, SMS (short messaging system). Twitter thus borrows the etiquette of SMS as both compressed and seemingly fleeting. While the information arrives faster, the quality of that information may be lower and less considered. Increasingly stories are noted as either Twitterable or not.

Some have also pointed out that the same factors that allow citizen journalism to challenge Big Media and established power structures can be utilised by these same groups to move Big Media into the internet age. Politicians, celebrities and large organisations are using blogs and social media in the same way as citizen journalists, presenting their own perspectives and views with the same level of apparent openness as any other citizen journalist. While this may not be a problem in and of itself, it undermines the contention that digital media is fundamentally empowering – it can also be used to reinforce, strengthen and deepen existing power structures.

As social media becomes more pervasive, it is also influencing the way we think about citizen journalism. Following their citizen journalism project based around the 2007 Australian election, Bruns et al. noted that there is a role for sites that facilitate 'communities of news and content makers', which suggests a new form of journalism that they tentatively refer to as 'journalism as social networking' (2009: 205). For them, this construction helps get around the unfruitful professional-versus-amateur issue that lies at the heart of much criticism of citizen journalism. They argue that an emergent 'networked journalism' would incorporate both trained journalists and citizen journalists, enjoying the strengths of both forms of news gathering and reportage.

ONLINE ACTIVISM

> Cyberspace has become a global electronic agora where the diversity of human disaffection explodes in a cacophony of accents. (Castells 2001: 138)

Citizen journalism is one specific form of produsage that is enabled by participative media, most notably in this case, blogs. Online activism is related in that it also enables various participative media, and allows produsers to express opinions and ideas in the online environment. Online activism goes beyond commentary – it allows groups of people to organise around a political issue.

What is online activism?

Online (or internet) activism is a burgeoning area, and has seen the publication of numerous books and articles on the subject. This presents a problem for researchers who are new to the area because it is hard to determine what the key texts are. As Garrett (2006) points out, the literature also comes at the same issue from different perspectives and fields, further complicating study. Our goal in this section is not to try to cover the entire gamut of online activism, because to do so would take us well away from social media and into other subjects that are only tangentially related. However, in order to examine the importance of participation, it would be remiss of us to ignore the importance of online activism and particularly its intersection with social media. By way of contextualising this section, let us briefly outline some of the fundamental points about online activism before going on to examine some examples and how social media has influenced online debates.

One of the earliest and best-known groups to use the internet for social activism was the Zapatistas, a revolutionary movement based in the Chiapas state of Mexico. In late 1993 the Zapatistas occupied a number of towns in southern Mexico, and gained attention in the West for their use of the internet as a means to communicate with the rest of the world. Although, as Turner (2005) points out, the Zapatistas come from an impoverished area of Mexico, they relied upon non-governmental organisations to place their hand-written materials onto the internet. In particular, they were supported by the San Francisco Institute of Global Communication, who Castells describes as 'an NGO of socially responsible "techies"' (2001: 138). They helped establish an internet network in Mexico called La Neta, which in turn supported the Zapatistas as well as a number of other activist groups in Mexico.

While the reality of how the Zapatistas got their messages online may dispel romantic images of revolutionaries writing emails from satellite-linked laptops in remote caves or jungle hideouts, it emphasises the growing impact of the internet for activists – even sometimes those working outside wired environments – to increase awareness about their cause. For Cleaver, the Zapatistas' approach to activism, including their use of the internet, 'has inspired and stimulated a wide variety of grassroots political efforts in many other countries', a phenomenon which Cleaver refers to as the 'Zapatista effect' (Cleaver 1998). As the quote at the beginning of this section suggests, Castells sees the internet as becoming a place where social disaffection is engaged on a global scale.

Online activism and a democratising internet

The study of online activism returns us to one of the fundamental claims about the internet: that it is inherently democratising. Some early writers claimed that the internet was democratic by its very design because, as John

Gilmore is famously quoted in a *Time International* article from 1993, the internet 'interprets censorship as damage and routes around it' (Elmer-Dewitt 1993). This suggests that the internet's physical architecture constitutes a kind of agora in which all ideas can be freely presented, and all people are free to engage with them. The idea of the agora is borrowed from the agora of ancient Greece. Agora were marketplaces where communities would come together to trade in goods and produce, but also to engage in politics and matters of public life. In the late 1960s the German sociologist Jürgen Habermas developed the concept of the public sphere, an agora-like conceptual space that he saw as an engine of social change that had been eroded by the emergence of mass media (Habermas 1989). Habermas's book was published in German in 1969 but was not translated into English until 1989, at which time it was well placed to provide a theoretical foundation to discussions of the internet and its potential relationship with democracy (Dahlgren 2001). Both Habermas's ideas of public sphere and the concept of the agora as a marketplace of ideas have figured prominently in debates about the role of the internet as a democratising social force.

The emergence of social media has only served to accentuate debate around the role of the internet in democratic processes and activism. As participative media has made it increasingly easy for people to create and share media, social media provides services that allow people to come together and organise around issues. With the growing ubiquity of internet-enabled mobile phones, these features of online activism can more readily be translated into offline contexts.

'Smart mobs' provide one example of the interface between social media and offline organisation (Rheingold 2002). The term 'smart mob' describes a large group of people who use mobile technologies as a way of connecting with each other, thus allowing the group to act with a kind of collective intelligence. Smart mobs can be organised online and can allow activists to organise protests with many people at short notice. One example often used to illustrate smart mobs is the way that mobile text messaging was used to organise protests in the Philippines against then President Joseph Estrada. Estrada was impeached in 2000 following allegations of corruption, and his trial was covered widely in the mass media. At one point the judges in the trial elected not to admit a critical piece of evidence. Outraged people took to the streets using their mobiles and text messaging to organise protests (in the Philippines, mobile call costs are high, while mobile texting is cheap and thus has a high level of use). Soon afterwards Estrada lost the support of the military and was ousted in a coup, replacing Estrada with the then vice-president Gloria Macapagal-Arroyo. These smart-mob protests, organised by text messaging, were credited with playing a significant role in the ousting of Estrada.

Examples of the use of the internet and social media in particular to organise social protests are increasingly easy to find. Social media has been implicated as playing a role in the so-called Arab Spring uprisings in the Middle East during 2011, and have played a prominent role in the Occupy movements in the US and other Western nations. The Arab Spring is a phrase that refers to the widespread social and political unrest that spread across the Middle East from December 2010. During this period anti-government and pro-democracy protesters ousted leaders in Yemen, Tunisia, Libya and Egypt, and significant protests erupted in numerous other countries in the region. It was widely reported that social media played a significant role in helping protesters to organise and share information in states where other forms of media are strictly regulated. Howard et al. (2011) analysed millions of social media posts from the period leading up to and throughout the Arab Spring in order to determine what, if any, effect social media had. They argued that social media played a key role in the Arab Spring uprisings, noting that tools like Twitter and Facebook were used by well-educated urban youth, many of them female, to pressure governments. They saw spikes in conversations that they described as 'revolutionary' just prior to major events, and suggest that social media helped to spread political dissent beyond the borders of countries.

Although social media is implicated in all of these movements, one of the persistent questions is exactly what role it plays. It seems unlikely that these technologies are the main cause or catalyst for social activism. As Anderson points out, countries like Egypt and Libya have a long history of social activism and protest that predates modern communication technologies (Anderson 2011). Another way of asking this question is whether online environments are purely instrumental, or whether they actually change the dynamics of activism, including the players, their goals and their methods (Castells 2001: 137). In many ways, online environments both are instrumental in, and change (or are indicative of change), the nature of activism. In the Arab Spring example, it seems likely that while social media played a role, it was an instrumental one, appropriated by a movement because of its utility, and abandoned when its utility was limited.

In other cases, as Castells argues, political movements are shaped by the structure of modern information societies; and the internet, as the emblematic expression of communication media in the information society, becomes an important organising site. Castells draws parallels between the labour movements of the nineteenth and early twentieth centuries and modern social movements. Where the labour movement extended from the factories and used pubs as rallying points, modern movements extend from the network and use the internet as their medium (Castells 2001: 139). For Castells, the social movements of the network society have certain common features. He points to anti-globalisation movements that are not highly structured organisations like the trade unions before them, and are in fact a conglomerate of various different groups with local and culturally inflected concerns that, through the internet, can coordinate their efforts. These movements are global, although they draw strength through local mobilisation.

The Occupy Wall Street movement is an example of a protest movement that extends from the network. Beginning in September 2011, this movement was designed to highlight the growing inequality in Western societies, emphasised by the global financial crisis and the protection that was extended to banks and financial institutions (whose questionable business decisions and loose ethics were heavily implicated in the crisis) by governments while individuals and families lost their homes and livelihood. Even before the first protests began, this movement was deeply linked to the internet, with a domain name for the protests registered in June of that year. A Facebook page appeared only days later. Like the Arab Spring protests, the Occupy movement used social media to organise people and provide a virtual rallying point for activists. For the Occupy movement, social media provides a site for a variety of very different and disconnected protest groups to come together and protest for a common cause.

It seems, then, that some movements, like the Arab Spring uprisings, might be said to be heavily based in local issues that are less about the new networked society and more about ongoing struggles expressed through different, multiple public channels. In these cases, social media appears as an instrumental tool, an implement that can be wielded by activists to enhance their activities. Other movements, like the anti-globalisation movement, arise from the networked society, and are shaped by the structure of the society, responding to its challenges and tensions. In this second case, the internet and social media suit the forms, methods and goals of the kinds of activism typical of anti-globalisation protests.

Problems with online activism

By way of another example, and in order to segue into some of the problems with social media-based activism, we now turn to an example that is intensely connected to social media, *Kony 2012*. In March 2012, as we were preparing this book, an activist group called Invisible Children Incorporated put a video on YouTube titled *Kony 2012*. The video, which was 24 minutes in length, featured a simple message that was reinforced by highly emotive content. The message was 'make Joseph Kony famous'. Joseph Kony is the leader of a paramilitary group called the LRA, which operated in Uganda and then moved into the surrounding countries. In 2005, Kony was indicted by the International Criminal Court for crimes against humanity. The idea behind the video was to bring popular attention to Kony's crimes and to drum up popular support for continued US military support of the Ugandan government's attempts to capture Kony.

The video was immediately shared by millions of people via Facebook and Twitter, and the YouTube video achieved over 40 million hits within the first few days of its launch, with the number continuing to climb past 84 million. Critical responses to the video followed, with a number of journalists, academics, Ugandans and organisations criticising the way the video simplified a complex problem, and, many claimed, contained misleading facts. The film was seen by some as a kind of neo-colonialism that depicted Ugandans as powerless, while others questioned the financial transparency of the Invisible Children organisation. These criticisms prompted Invisible Children Inc. to publish a response to the critiques.[2]

Questions about the finances and backing of online activists, as raised in the criticisms of *Kony 2012*, suggest more fundamental issues with the transparency of online activist organisations. As we identified earlier, social media allows campaigns to be organised very quickly, and the combination of affective social networks and well-designed rich media (for example, video materials) can evoke action (even if it is in the form of making a financial donation to a cause) before people have had time to properly assess the cause. This was the case with *Kony 2012*, and will no doubt be the case for similar causes into the future. This is not to say that such causes are not worthy of support, but merely to point to some of the problems that stem from slick marketing-inspired campaigns that encourage action without thought.

The *Kony 2012* video is a powerful demonstration of how effective social media can be for groups with the right skills and knowledge to get a message out to millions of people very quickly and raise the profile of a cause. However, the immediate controversy around the video and its use of social media raise some very salient questions about the role of social media in social activism. In particular, it raises serious questions about the value of social media in creating a new kind of activism in which participants feel good because they have taken a stance, but in fact may have done very little, and may actually do harm. The problems facing central Africa are significant, and cannot easily be reduced to a 24-minute YouTube video, or a trite one-line campaign message. Support for the video is not the same thing as support for a movement.

This kind of activism has pejoratively been described as 'slacktivism' to denote activism that is lazy, half-hearted and generally 'slack'. Others point to the emergence of online activist groups who use social media and online marketing techniques as a way of engaging social media users with political movements. The word 'clicktivism' has been coined to describe 'the pollution of activism with the logic of consumerism' (www.clicktivism.org). Critics argue that this undermines traditional modes of activism and constitutes a threat to movements that require more substantial engagement from activists.

In Australia, for example, GetUp was established as an online site that bills itself as '[a]n independent movement to build a progressive Australia and bring participation back into our democracy' (www.getup.org.au). The site allows people to vote for causes that GetUp will back if they achieve sufficient popularity. Thus, 'ordinary Australians' can feel they are engaging politically and making a difference by signing up to digital petitions or voting for causes that matter to them. Whether this constitutes true activism or not is open to debate, but it does suggest the evolution of new avenues for political activism with unusual topologies (Flew and Wilson 2010).

CONCLUSION

In this chapter we have looked at participation as a central concept that underlies social media. The internet has always been a two-way medium that supports the production of digital content by anyone with internet access. However, social media has enabled and encouraged participation by making the production, distribution and storage of content less challenging and, in many cases, all but free. Emergent from this phenomenon is the user who produces – the phenomenon that Bruns (2005, 2008) has helpfully described as the 'produser'. However, it is important to ask how much 'produsing' is repurposed for profit by the companies such as Google and Facebook, and at what point does this repurposing become problematic, especially when weighed against the potential value of the material being produced?

The examples of produsage illustrated in this chapter – crowd sourcing, Wikipedia, citizen journalism and online activism – demonstrate some of the ways that produsage is impacting on how we engage not only with the internet but also with society itself. This provides yet another context for both of our central themes. Participation reinforces the importance of offline realities in online behaviour. Far from developing new forms of expression that are disconnected from the real world, people's online productive behaviour is strongly anchored in real-world concerns. For Salam Pax, blogging from inside Iraq during the Gulf War, participative media allowed his very local and contextualised perspective to transcend the informational controls of both the Hussein regime and the mainstream Western media to provide readers from around the world with a strong and personal connection to something very real that had ramifications well beyond the digital world.

While produsage – particularly in forms such as online activism and citizen journalism – appears to be a very empowering use of social media, there are always issues around exploitation, as we saw in Chapter 3. We must be careful to bring a critical eye to any claims of revolutionary change. Although citizen journalism promises empowerment through a more open press that avoids the bottlenecks and gatekeeping of Big Media, it also raises issues about transparency, trust and quality. Online activism provides exciting opportunities for democratic participation and change even in places where political dissent is treated harshly, but it also opens up potentials for the abuse of good intentions. The participative dimensions of social media are subject to local conditions, highlighting that what constitutes 'participation' is defined by the forces of the local environment.

NOTES

1 *David after the Dentist* became a hit on the internet when it was posted in 2009. See www.youtube.com/watch?v=txqiwrbYGrs.
2 www.invisiblechildren.com.s3-website-us-east-1.amazonaws.com/critiques.html.

5 Art and cultural production

As we saw in the previous chapter, social media has opened up new avenues for participation in many areas of social life, and is having an immediate and visible impact in fields like journalism and social activism. In this chapter we want to look at the ways that these same changes, both represented and exacerbated by social media and the concomitant rise of user created content (UCC), are *effecting* and *affecting* the production of other cultural products. In this chapter we will be focusing on the way that social media is both challenging the arts while, at the same time, providing artists with new avenues for artistic expression. Although much has been written about the adaptation and remediation of other media like television and film via online media, the role of art and social media has been relatively overlooked (Perkel 2012).

This chapter explores two major trajectories. First, we look at the ways that cultural institutions like museums and galleries are responding to the challenges of evidence-based policy and social media by embracing the concepts of Web 2.0 in order to engage with their visitors. We briefly outline some of the main points about internet art and its status in the art establishment prior to social media. This is important because it demonstrates how the arts have responded to the development of the internet, and sets the scene for the rise of social media. Second, we look at how the traditional domination of culture by these institutions is being eroded as new and old forms of creativity are being revealed by social media, and we consider the impact of social media on cultural institutions – which we define here as museums and galleries. After looking at how these traditional arbiters of culture have responded to social media, we look at how artists are responding to social media. Here we identify that the tensions felt by cultural institutions are also being engaged with by artists in a variety of ways. Finally, we will examine the rise of art websites, with a particular focus on deviantART (as an example of an art-based SNS) and its role as an alternative to traditional cultural institutions as arbiters of culture. Following on from this discussion, we will finish the chapter by engaging with Burgess's notion of vernacular creativity (2007) and the rise in importance of everyday situated creativity, not just in art, but in social relations more broadly.

CULTURAL PRODUCTION

To begin, it is important to be clear about what we mean by the term 'cultural production'. The term 'culture' is highly loaded in academic literature and has been studied to a great degree from many different perspectives. Rather than trying to present a single unified definition of culture here, we will take a particular perspective on culture that we draw from the academic traditions of critical theory and cultural studies. These traditions are particularly relevant for an engagement with cultural production concerning the media (and here we include the internet) because the media has often been a focus of their study.

Critical theory is a branch of sociology that is associated with the Frankfurt School, a group of leftist scholars who worked in Germany prior to the Second World War. These scholars, writing in the 1920s and 1930s, included people like Max Horkheimer, Theodor Adorno and Walter Benjamin, although the tradition extends past the War and into the 1960s to include others like Herbert Marcuse and Jürgen Habermas. These scholars wrote on a number of issues, but their most well-known works concern the relationship between culture and capitalist society. Writing from the 1930s, before television and during the heyday of radio and the early days of commercial cinema, the Frankfurt School scholars were witnessing a great deal of social upheaval in Germany as Adolf Hitler and the Nazi party began making their move into power. The importance of radio and its use by the Nazi party for propaganda was significant at this time. As Jews and intellectuals, many of the Frankfurt School scholars fled Nazi Germany and moved to the US where they continued their writings.

Much could (and has) been written about the Frankfurt School, but for our purposes here, we want to focus on one of the most famous essays that came out of the Frankfurt School, titled 'The Culture Industry', written by Max Horkheimer and Theodore Adorno in 1944. In this essay, Adorno and Horkheimer described the culture industries as being akin to heavy, factory-based industry. Commercial radio, newspapers and cinema were factories that produced culture for the purposes of manipulation of the masses in the pursuit of consumerism and/or fascism. They distinguished between high culture (like fine art, for example), which they felt encouraged thinking and critical engagement, and low culture, which they saw as base-level entertainment pumped out by the culture industries. This low culture was easy for people to access and enjoy, but also acted as a kind of tranquiliser that provided people with distraction and built demand for goods that they didn't really need.

This notion of the media as all-powerful cultural industries remained prominent until the late 1970s. As discussed in Chapter 4, Hall's seminal *Encoding and Decoding in the Television Discourse* (1973), in which he argued that the meaning in a media text (a TV show or a film, for example) is not necessarily fixed but is open to active interpretation by the viewer, started a radical rethinking of this model. Hall's restructuring of dynamics between the reader/audience and text can also been seen earlier in the highly influential work of Roland Barthes, particularly in his concept of the 'death of the author' (1966 [1977]) in which he pronounced the 'birth of the reader' as an active participant in the process of making meaning. The encoding/ decoding nexus opened a new chapter on the study of the culture industries, because although the culture industries could produce culture with an intention, the reader/viewer/listener was free to interpret that content as they wished. Later cultural theorists developed a circular model – such as the circuit of culture (Du Gay et al. 1997) – where the culture industries were themselves subject to the meanings constructed by audiences. In other words, through things like TV ratings and audience analysis, the culture industries modified their production of culture to better suit their target markets. This general approach to studying cultural production (one in which the audience plays a crucial role in the construction of meaning) has become known as 'cultural studies', and now includes a range of different ideas and theories, and forms an important scholarly basis for many internet studies.

From this perspective, cultural production is about the way that culture is produced and reproduced within modern societies. Culture here can be in the form of media texts (television programmes, podcasts, websites, films) or cultural objects (iPods, mobile phones and so on). Horkheimer and Adorno saw cultural production as a mass industry, with factories producing easy-to-swallow culture to be consumed by the masses in order to keep them controlled (and consuming). For Hall and cultural studies, the focus has shifted from production to consumption as the point at which meaning is made. With this shift in focus also comes a shift in the focus of study: from the political economy of large organisations and how they make cultural products, to the uses of cultural products and how people construct meaning in everyday life.

With the rise of the internet and especially more recently with the rise of Web 2.0 and participative media, cultural-studies scholars have found themselves in familiar territory. As discussed in Chapter 4, people are now producing and distributing of their own original media texts that are in turn being consumed by other people. The dominance of centralised production is apparently being eroded by new kinds of decentralised production, and this raises all kinds of questions about the emerging role of social media in modern societies.

Chapter 4 examined some of the ramifications of this in the realm of journalism and political activism, but how does it translate to the realm of cultural production? What impacts does UCC have upon the individuals and organisations that have traditionally been the arbiters of culture? What new possibilities does it open for these individuals and organisations? There are many different ways to examine these questions, because there are many different ways that culture is produced in the emerging social media landscape. We could look, for example, at the ways in which independent film is changing in the face of cheaper production technologies and internet video-sharing sites like YouTube or Vimeo. We could examine the impact that social media and distribution portals like the iPhone's app store has on the way that software (until recently rather neglected as cultural objects) is produced.

Rather than engaging with a grab-bag of different examples of cultural production, in the following sections we are going to examine cultural production from the perspective of the arts. The arts are interesting to us here because they have traditionally been the site for the production of culture and the identification of what is considered culturally significant and what is not. Public institutions such as museums and galleries have long been the arbiters of taste, defining what is and what is not culturally significant, and now these institutions are having to respond to a more interactive public and be more demonstrably accountable to them, thanks in part to social media. As social media provides new ways for artists to connect with people and to sell their work (we will consider deviantART below), the role of private galleries in the art market is also being challenged. Art historian Julian Stallabrass notes that social media poses a serious challenge to the authority of arts institutions. He writes, '[t]o the extent that online art is associated with the culture of Web 2.0 and the "wealth of networks", it appears not merely dissociated from the mainstream market for contemporary art but dangerous to it' (Stallabrass 2010: 7).

In the post-dotcom world, and with the rise of social media, we are seeing an expansion in the variety of cultural production, and at the same time we are seeing a diminution in the traditional roles of institutions (whether they are giant media companies or public institutions) in dictating what are and are not considered valuable cultural materials. In the following sections we will examine the impact of social media on art and cultural production at different levels. We begin by looking at how cultural institutions have responded to social media and what is perceived as a focus on the interactive audience.

CULTURAL INSTITUTIONS AND SOCIAL MEDIA

> Both museums and galleries are committed to the mystification of the objects
> that they display, holding to the fiction of a distinct realm of high art that
> stands above the bureaucratised world of work and the complementary vulgar
> blandishments of mass culture. (Stallabrass 2010: 7)

The term 'cultural institution' has been used to describe a wide range of
organisations that produce or are involved in the production of culture
under a broad definition that includes the cultural industries (such as radio,
television and film), schools and education. Here, though, we are mainly
concerned with public institutions that have traditionally been the arbiters
of culture – museums, galleries and libraries. When we use the term 'cultural
institution' in this chapter, we are referring to these organisations. Keep in
mind, however, that many of the points we make about museum, galleries
and libraries also apply to other cultural industries.

Cultural institutions, whether they be galleries, museums or libraries,
have traditionally mediated the relationship between the art/artefact and
the public. Whether public or commercial, the role of the gallery is to act
as a filter, choosing a subset of works and presenting them to the visitor/
viewer/reader. The idea of selection is vitally important here – what gets
selected (and what gets excluded) by an institution makes explicit claims
about the cultural values of the institution, which in turn reflects and potentially reinforces or constructs the culture of a society. Traditionally, art and
culture that is selected and included in this way can be referred to as 'high
culture', whereas cultural productions that are common, everyday or folk
art are considered 'low culture'.

Art institutions have played a key role in normalising tastes and aesthetics associated with 'art'. Even when the content of art brings traditionally
non-art content or values into the gallery (like avant-garde movements such
as 'relational aesthetics'), ultimately the role of these spaces in orchestrating
taste cultures only seems to be reinforced. Relational aesthetics is defined
by the French art critic Nicolas Bourriaud as 'a set of artistic practices
which take as their theoretical and practical point of departure the whole
of human relations and their social context, rather than an independent and
private space' (Bourriaud 2002: 113). Artists who engage in this kind of art
practice will stage an event in which the experience of the event is the artwork, rather than objects hanging in a gallery. The point is to displace the
gallery and even the artist from the art. An example is Rirkrit Tiravanija's
untitled show in 1992 where he invited people into a gallery and cooked
them Thai food. The art here was the environment and experience of that
environment created by the food, the people and the cooking: the art is the

experience that emerges from relationships between the real-world experiences of eating, talking and anything else that goes on in that place at that time. The problem with relational aesthetics in practice is that the events in many cases simply reinforce the role of the artist (making them into mini-celebrities hosting the event) and bring attention and fame to the gallery hosting the event. Art institutions, therefore, continue to maintain a strong role in defining art even in the face of a movement that attempts to undermine that.

Bourdieu, whose work we discussed in Chapter 3 in relation to social capital, was one of the key sociologists to explore the construction and naturalisation of taste through various forms of culture – from art to films to television (1984 [1979]). Rather than focus upon class, Bourdieu's analysis of 'taste' provided a productive vehicle for understanding the then contemporary formations of aesthetics. In his analysis of 1,200 French people in the 1970s, Bourdieu defined three key types of knowledge he called 'capital': social, economic and cultural. While social capital was defined by who you know rather than what you know (that is, social connections), cultural capital was defined by education, background and some of the more tacit aspects of lifestyle. Institutions like museums and galleries play a role in establishing and defining cultural capital. However, with the rise of Web 2.0, questions about the role of museums as arbiters of taste have begun to arise as they become but one of many contexts for art production and consumption. In particular, we must ask just how much Web 2.0 ideologies, which emphasise the importance of fostering collaboration and sharing, reinforce or subvert traditional notions of authorship, taste and creativity.

THE CHANGING ROLE OF CULTURAL INSTITUTIONS

As Huhtamo (2002) observes, many twentieth-century avant-garde ('advance guard') movements such as futurism and Dadaism challenged the role of art galleries and exhibitions as arbiters for definitions of art. For example, father of the ready-made, Marcel Duchamp, was a keen provocateur. Through using a commercially made, banal and everyday object as his art, Duchamp challenged the limits of debates around art's content and craftsmanship. By taking, for example, a urinal, and rotating it 90 degrees, signing it (with a pseudonym) and placing it in a gallery, Duchamp challenged the limits of art and, especially, the role of the gate-keepers of the art world. Duchamp's play with the relationship between context and content, which would haunt much of twentieth-century art (especially minimalism), moved art from the world of safe craftsmanship, value judgements and aesthetics into the messy world of concepts. Duchamp's challenges around context and content, while still very much present in questions about the limits of contemporary art, become even more amplified in an age of social media.

The changes that started to take place in galleries and museums in the early twentieth century were also about shifting the role of the viewer – a phenomenon which still continues today. For example, in relational aesthetics we described above, the viewer becomes an active participant in the making of the experience and meanings. Unquestionably informing the ground-breaking work of Roland Barthes in 'The death of the author' (1966 [1977]), in which he argues that the role of readers to interpret makes them as active in the meanings as the author, many early twentieth-century avant-garde movements – especially conceptualism – sought to construct the viewer as an active maker of both meaning and, in some cases, the actual artwork. These debates about agency and participation resonate with the texture of Web 2.0 as supporting collaboration, participation and UCC. Given this, could we not view UCC as this century's ready-made?

The role of the museum or gallery has been inverted, and context has increasingly been eradicated from museum and gallery spaces so that people are free to engage with the artworks without cultural interference from things like the classical architectural features that dominated Victorian galleries. As Huhtamo remarks, 'instead of a passive spectator in front of static exhibits, the visitor is meant to turn into an active participant' (2002: 6). For David Fleming, Director of National Museums Liverpool, the main thing that characterises change in the twenty-first-century museum is their relationship with what he calls their 'audience':

> essentially there is little that is totally new in museums activity beyond a massive change in our attitude towards audiences, which might best be described as one of total inclusion, that is of all the public, not just a narrow sector. (Fleming 2005: 6)

Now the 'active participant' that Huhtamo referred to is being recast as the 'interactive participant' as various factors come to push for a change in the way that cultural institutions engage with the public. Chief among these concerns is the ongoing democratisation of cultural institutions that, as we have described, has been an ongoing concern throughout the twentieth century. The second is that since the 1980s, as governments started placing more faith in market forces, cultural institutions have been required to justify their funding by showing how effectively and efficiently they are engaging with the public.

Cultural institutions in the age of social media

In this climate, the rise of social media affords new ways for public arts institutions to engage with their visitors (and quantify this engagement). Arts institutions such as museums and public galleries have embraced social media, seeing it as a way to reach out to the community and involve them in order to both improve access and improve understanding. This represents a shift towards a user-focused conceptualisation of public arts institutions that can be compared to the kind of shift that O'Reilly characterises as occurring in the internet's move from Web 1.0 to Web 2.0 (2005).

It is perhaps not surprising that the Web 2.0 mantra has been picked up with alacrity by arts institutions, with terms like 'Museums 2.0' (Simon 2012) and 'Art 2.0' (Broun 2007) being used as direct invocations of O'Reilly's formulation. Here public arts institutions are turning to the logic of Web 2.0 and applying that to their relationship with visitors both online and in the physical museums. Elizabeth Broun, director of the Smithsonian American Art Museum, sees the development of the online aspect of public art institutions as an imperative:

> There is really no way any longer for public museums and libraries to separate their bricks and mortar business from their virtual business. They have to integrate with each other, and it is no longer optional to do these things. It is now required. (Broun 2007)

This is a telling statement. It both represents the reality of modern arts institutions in the US, the UK and Australia as business-like institutions, as well as emphasising the perceived importance of online media in supporting the interactive visitor. For Broun, the 'virtual' museum is not just a valuable concept, it is *required*. For public arts institutions the integration of online and offline aspects has resulted in numerous different approaches, from the development of virtual museums and galleries, which makes collections available for online viewing from the comfort of one's home, to the use of the social media techniques, such as folksonomy (a portmanteau of 'folk' and 'taxonomy', meaning a classification system generated by the general public), in order to engage people with collections.

An example of a virtual gallery is Art Project, a collaboration between a number of galleries and Google. The project uses Google's Streetview technology to take users on an unguided tour through the art galleries that participate in the project. High-resolution images of individual paintings can be clicked on, zoomed in and then accessed to obtain more detailed information about the artwork. Users can then use their Google account to create an 'artwork collection' which can be shared using Google's SNS Google+, so neatly integrating the online experience into the social network. This is not just about making the gallery available online; it is also about utilising social media in order to encourage people to engage with the galleries.

Despite their technological 'wow' factor, the value of the virtual gallery is debatable. While they provide access to the images of the gallery, they do not necessarily engage the viewer in the same way as a physical space. For Australian artist Anastasia Klose, the physicality of the gallery space is important:

> YouTube, MySpace and the Internet in general is no substitute for a gallery. But it can offer a good resource for people wanting to research an artist ... The gallery space is transformative, powerful and singular. Being able to physically experience an artwork (video or otherwise), i.e. 'see it' in all its non-compressed glory, is paramount. Seeing documentation, or video excerpts online, is no substitute. (Klose, 2011)

Virtual galleries are, however, only one of the ways through which museums are utilising social media. Many museums and galleries are using social media in order to encourage a kind of crowd-sourced grass-roots curatorial role for users. Here, the idea of curators as experts who can put together a single unified exhibition of (say) sixteenth-century tapestry is replaced with a model where the general public are encouraged to build their own pathways through a collection. The role of the curator does not disappear, but does change. In the examples of virtual galleries above, social media plays an important role.

Many museums are now making their collection databases available online for public access, and in many cases are providing interactive ways for people to engage with the collections through the web. The use of folksonomies is one example of how exposing databases on the web allows people to become more involved with public art institutions – in this case, encouraging people to become curators. Folksonomies, as the name suggests, are crowd-sourced taxonomies, essentially asking large numbers of people to associate keywords or 'tags' with objects. Over time, and with enough people tagging objects, new ways of presenting and organising objects within a collection can be determined through a crowd-sourced index. This allows people to 'assert their own connections and associations between objects in ways that reflect personal perspectives and interests' (Trant 2006: 85).

The Commons on Flickr, for example, is a collection of images uploaded by different museums and galleries from around the world. Users can browse the image collections, which, by virtue of being in the Flickr SNS, can be tagged and marked, shared by users and even accessed through the

Flickr API, allowing people to create software applications that incorporate images from the Commons. Numerous software applications have been developed to take advantage of the Commons materials, allowing the photos to be sorted and presented to viewers in a range of ways. The Flickr Commons Explorer, for example, is a software application that lets users explore Commons collections. The software can be downloaded from the internet, and when run it loads up images from the various collections, presenting an interface to the viewer that lets them browse and isolate images by keywords in their titles. This software provides an example of how museums are harnessing social media techniques to increase participation with their collections (Hinton and Whitelaw 2010).

Cultural institutions are turning to social media in a response to economic pressures and the changing demands of the audience. Instead of using experts to select the works that are considered important or noteworthy, expertise is increasingly being used to help visitors navigate the collections and develop their own exhibitions and pathways through the material. This is displacing the primacy of cultural institutions as the absolute arbiters of culture, or at least is changing their role so that there is a more dynamic understanding of culture emerging.

ART AND SOCIAL MEDIA

If cultural institutions have embraced social media, then the response to social media from professional artists and the arts community at large has been mixed. While some artists have been reluctant to engage with social media, either through Luddism or genuine resistance, others have been quick to embrace what they see as a way to get their work out to larger audiences. Some have gone so far as to claim that social media is the new gallery, arguing that artists should use social media as a platform to market and sell their work. At the same time, new artists are emerging through online art communities such as deviantART, which provides a way for emerging and non-traditional artists to gain attention and potentially financial benefit from their work outside of the traditional structures of the art world.

Artists and social media

One of the ways that artists have responded to social media is to make art from social media itself. Artists use social media in different ways: having their work influenced by input from social media like Twitter; producing visual works based on social networks and online interactions; and performing within social media as a platform for delivering art and reflecting on the medium in which it is delivered.

Figure 5.1 Anastasia Klose, *My boyfriend dumped me on Facebook* (2007), C-type photograph

Figure 5.2 Anastasia Klose, *Facebook ruined my life* (2007), C-type photograph

Man Bartlett is a New-York-based artist who used Twitter in a number of performance pieces. The works involve Bartlett occupying a space and sending messages to Twitter. In his first project, Bartlett spent 24 hours in Union

Square Best Buy (a convenience store) where he didn't buy anything. His tweets told people what he was doing, thinking and looking at, and for the 24 hours he remained engaged in thoughts about buying. While Bartlett has attracted a great deal of attention for his use of social media in his performance pieces, his work raises questions about the nature of internet art in the age of social media. For example, how important is interaction with the audience to the performance, and if it is important, then what is the role of the artist, and to what extent does the work become a collaboration with Bartlett as just one of the participants?

An Xiao (2010) is a social media artist who engaged with some of these questions in a round-table she convened with some other social media artists in 2009. One of the questions she asked them was, What is social media art? As a result of the discussion, she defined social media art as consisting of four 'rules of thumb'. She says that, first, social media art is art where the web plays a key role in the expression of the art; it is not enough for the work to be marketed on the web, nor that it is sourced from the web. Second, the art must involve the audience somehow because social media is a social medium. Third, she says that the work must be accessible to an audience outside the art world, but must still be conceptually rich. Fourth, social media art is about intent – the artist must be able to articulate a reason or purpose of the artwork that then permits it to be examined and validated by others.

What's interesting in Xiao's conceptualisation of social media art is that a clear notion of a divide between the artist and the audience must exist, suggesting tensions between the privileged position of the artist as a specialist, and the untrained. However, as we saw in Chapters 2 and 4, the rise in UCC practices is having profound effects on traditional modes of knowledge and cultural production and is blurring the lines between the producer and consumer. The question is whether artists can maintain their privileged position, and if not, what does this mean for the symbiosis of art, culture and technology?

As the internet continues to become more mainstream, the concept of 'internet art' as a separate art form may well decline. From some perspectives the Candy Factory (Styled as *CANDY FACTORY PROJECTS), a Japanese group consisting of collaborations with artists from elsewhere, encapsulates the spirit of this by deploying collaboration and the visual economy of repetition often associated with the visuality of the internet. Much like their frequent collaborative partners Young-Hae Chang Heavy Industries, whose visual aesthetics seem to be a reminder of early web animated graphics, the Candy Factory deploys an aesthetic and ideological position that is a cornerstone of Web 2.0. For the Candy Factory's Takuji

Kogo, the web-inspired aesthetics of the work bleed into the gallery space, and the relationship between online art and offline art is blurred:

> More recently I often present images as looped and mirrored or still images animated through close-ups and pan shots. I see them as looped video sculptures that function both for the exhibition space and online. I have also been engaged in several collaborative projects working with different subject matter and material using the same techniques. I've been trying to utilize *CANDY FACTORY PROJECTS as a sort of software which can be used as a platform of diverse collaborations. (Kogo, 2011)

The Candy Factory both mirrors the composition of new media as well as adapting it back into the traditional context of art, the gallery. Kogo's use of the Candy Factory Project as a platform for collaboration echoes the way that SNSs are utilised as a platform for sociality, as discussed in Chapter 3. This adaptation of their work into traditional forms and offline spaces emphasises that the Candy Factory artists do not see themselves as internet artists, but as artists who use the internet. For Kogo, the importance of the internet needs to be understood in relation to offline considerations:

> Since diverse collaborations online are related to the planning of offline activities like the direction of Kitakyushu Biennial (which was organised by Candy Factory), neither is especially more important than the other. However, the web is free by definition from geographical constraints and I can anticipate an audience that has a wider spectrum of interests in genres other than only art. (Kogo, 2011)

The internet here is seen mainly as a way to engage with audiences over a wider geographical area. This is not to diminish the extra affordances that the internet presents to artists as the various contexts, content and genres afforded by this medium provide not only bigger audiences but also feedback into the collaborative nature of *CANDY FACTORY'S PROJECTS. The value of using the internet for art, however, is not seen by Kogo as remarkable or extraordinary. Indeed, Candy Factory artists feel uncomfortable with titles such as 'internet artists', preferring instead to see themselves as just 'artists'. Their use of internet themes and aesthetics reminds us that creativity and new media are both frequently borrowed from older modes of visuality as they simultaneously expand into new ones.

Beijing-based artist Cao Fei is another internet artist whose concerns and intentions are firmly anchored in the offline, but who uses the internet as a medium for engagement, performance and display. Cao Fei's art is embedded within the political reality of modern China and the Chinese government's complex and deeply conflicted relationship with the internet. China's government recognises the internet as being important for national development, but also as presenting a threat to the tight centralised control over the media and communications that they currently exercise. Thus the internet is not banned in China, although it is highly regulated. This tension has led to the implementation of the so-called Great Firewall of China, a technical and human system designed to block and censor the parts of the internet that are seen by the government as destabilising. For example, in 2009, with the twentieth anniversary of the Tiananmen Square massacre and the subsequent ethnic riots taking place in China, 'Western' media such as Facebook and Twitter were banned. Alternative social media services – carefully sanitised versions of SNSs like Facebook (Renren) and YouTube (Douban) – have been created, supported and controlled by the government. In this environment, the use of social media tools by artists is often blocked or hampered.

It is into this internet context that Cao Fei's work is presented. For her, the internet is another space for popular cultures in which local and global images and ideologies are up for reappropriation. Cao Fei's practice draws upon the various popular cultural references (hip hop, karaoke, cosplaying and so on) from Taiwan, Japan, Hong Kong and Hollywood. However, her perspective is informed by the way in which technologies and the internet have functioned in China as it shifted from communism to capitalism. Indeed, the visual culture of the internet in China is one informed by the particular politics of the local and governmental. She says:

> China's Great Fire Wall, or 'Great Firewall', for Internet information control is escalating. It is due to China's specific national conditions. What we can get is all 'restricted', limited, and incomplete. As Chinese, we are forced to accept the reality. Fortunately, we can use Second Life ... Currently, the Internet provides a new public space for exchanging our feelings. The Internet plays a good role in venting and consoling. Increasingly people hope this personal, intimate space can permeate the public life. The problem in the current Internet age is, it is a society under siege and every separated individual needs sympathy in a broader level. (Cao Fei 2011)

While Cao Fei's media practice would be perhaps less politically remarkable in other countries, within the Chinese technoscape her work takes on a much more politically charged element, something that is highlighted by her Second Life work, *RMB City*. Second Life is an online virtual world that is loosely based on the imaginings of science fiction writers such as William Gibson and Neal Stephenson and their respective concepts of cyberspace and the metaverse. Within Second Life, people, represented by a 3-D avatar, can walk around an online space populated by other people, buying, selling, building and creating. While once the darling of artists and the media, many are beginning to view Second Life with suspicion as it became little more than a corporate playground. However, within the technoscape of China, working in Second Life provides a space that is not (yet) under the same governmental controls as other internet media, as Cao Fei explains:

> Unfortunately, all the popular international social networking sites, like Facebook, YouTube, Vimeo, MySpace and Twitter, are currently prohibited in China. I have accounts for all the above social networking sites, but I can't use them now. They seem to be restricted areas which are abandoned and can't been seen. They are close to me but not available. Now I continue to run my own blog and the *RMB City* project in Second Life ... The network is a very attractive popular platform. As an *RMB City* cultural art project based on the internet community, Second Life 3-D, it is a work not only for browsing or surfing in the internet but also for operation. It will encourage and invite people to participate – raising questions and assumptions in its systematic construction. It presents an ideal that the future will be more open. (Cao Fei 2011)

Within *RMB City*, Cao Fei takes on the form of her avatar, China Tracy, who presents us with a pastiche of contemporary Chinese popular culture. In the virtual space of Second Life, *RMB City* presents as a playful and performative world where Pandas mix with MTV references in a space that mingles the popular with Cao Fei's own offline life and history. Cao Fei notes

Figure 5.3 Cao Fei/China Tracy, *RMB City: A Second Life City Planning* (2009)

that as an artist, the internet intensifies and complicates the artist's relationship with his or her audience:

> The power for connection is not only infinite and creative, but also subversive and destructive. I think that is a paradox. When finishing an artistic creation, the artist wishes it to be independent and subjective. At the same time, they also hope to receive public attention and response. The Internet as a medium provides a good model for interaction. But it depends on how the artist understands and handles its so-called 'open borders'. (Cao Fei 2011)

For Cao Fei, there is the dissolution of the barrier between visual art and new media practice, so that using new media and making art become similar things. Her position de-privileges the artist, or makes artists of us all:

> The world is multiplying and becoming cheaper to access. It is impossible for one culture to dominate another anymore. This is an information age. During this period, art can be communicated, copied and connected immediately. So it is more important that art can maintain its openness and sharing. I have uploaded a lot of video on to YouTube while many artists still only agree to put their works in the gallery or keep their works in limited access and not easily reproduced. *RMB* is in Flickr. You can find a lot of people to do some recording and sharing. I think these are the aesthetic characteristics of this era: 'Communication, sharing, created by a lot of people.' (Cao Fei 2011)

deviantART

In a great deal of the discussion within the arts community, art and artists are seen as a privileged elite, who produce art which is consumed by people – an audience – in much the same way that mass media produce content for audiences. As we have seen, for some artists (particularly those engaging with social media and the internet) the notion of the audience is becoming unclear as the boundaries between practice and art blur. However, in the mainstream art world, the clear division between artist and audience remains. The US National Endowment for the Arts report's title *Audience 2.0* sets the tone. This report tells us how people – 'the audience' – use the internet to participate in the arts. Participation here is generally not conceived as active construction of art works. Art is created by artists and presented to audiences in venues like galleries and theatres (National Endowment for the Arts 2010). Participation in this context implies watching or listening, but rarely active creation.

Yet as we have seen, social media is raising questions about the role and nature of the professional artist as a privileged source of culturally significant creative production. One of the consequences of the shifts in media paradigms from twentieth-century 'packaged' media to twenty-first-century 'conversational' media (Jenkins 2006) is that notions of authorship, creativity and collaboration have become part of everyday culture, rather than remaining in the hands of the elite. The art world is not immune to these transformations. We are now seeing the emergence of a range of creative activities that are produced by people who often do not see themselves as artists.

There are a number of websites that provide forums for painters, photographers, musicians and other artists to present their work. deviantART is an SNS platform that is themed around art. The word 'deviantART' refers to an idea that the site's artistic content is not officially sanctioned art, but instead deviates from the mainstream. The site's main purpose is summarised on its 'About' page:

> As a community destination, deviantART is a platform that allows emerging and established artists to exhibit, promote, and share their works within a *peer community dedicated to the arts*. The site's vibrant social network environment receives over 100,000 daily uploads of *original art works* ranging from traditional media, such as painting and sculpture, to digital art, pixel art, films and anime. (http://about.deviantART.com, original emphasis)

The site has 20 million registered members (called 'deviants'), some of whom sell their works online or who have established themselves in the commercial or art world as artists. The vast majority, though, are people who do not draw an income from their work and have no standing within the arts community. These others, the vast majority of those on the site, are home hobbyists, students and fan artists. The site provides a number of typical SNS features: each user maintains a profile, has a journal that they can use to post short messages, and supports a friends' list. The site also allows members to 'watch' other members, which provides a method for users to follow other users whose work they like. This is a similar concept to followers in Twitter and differs from friends in that a friend relationship is two-way and must be acknowledged by both parties.

The heart of the site, however, revolves around the idea of uploaded artworks – 'deviations' – which were initially images, but have evolved to encompass video as well. At the time of writing, the site claimed to have 197 million pieces of uploaded artworks. Individual users upload art to their sites where it is hosted and made publicly available for other users and non-users to see. Each artwork uploaded to the site can be commented on by others, allowing for community discussion to evolve around the topic of the artworks. The comments often consist of constructive criticism as more experienced users provide tips and advice to less experienced users.

Almila Akdag Salah (2010) compares deviantART to the Salon des Refusés, the gallery established by Napoleon III in 1863 for art works that were refused by French Academy Salons. For Salah, deviantART provides a tangible site that engages with some of the key questions in art today: the identity of the artist, the role of institutions and the status of collaborative art. The identity of the artist refers to how an artist is defined within the art community, both in terms of the kind of artist they are and in terms of their status as an artist. Salah identifies the 'identity politics' movement in the 1980s art world in which any difference (such as, gender and race) resulted in artists being labelled and pigeon-holed as 'minority' artists. This labelling profited some artists, but for many it operated as a handicap and limited readings of their work. Thus, an artist who is defined as an Australian Aboriginal artist is expected to produce works of art that are consistent with their aboriginality. This 'exoticisation' led to debates around the changing relationship between art and anthropology (Marcus and Myers 1995) whereby art critic Hal Foster (1996) proposed the artist as 'ethnographer'. In the online environment of deviantART, artists define themselves through a peer community, and so are freed somewhat from this form of discrimination and vertical labelling through curators and art buyers.

The second point that Salah makes about identity is perhaps more fundamental in the context of this chapter. She notes that identity also applies to the identity of the artist as an artist. This argument goes to a more fundamental question about what it is that defines an artist and the separation between artist and non-artist, a direct representation of the amateur/professional division that troubles other professions like journalists, as we saw in Chapter 4.

In an SNS such as deviantART, it becomes possible to develop quantitative measures of the relative popularity of individual users by tracking the number of people visiting their pages, making comments on their works and watching them. deviantART also regularly highlights the work of individual members of the community through the 'daily deviation', where anyone in the deviantART community can nominate a work to be featured. The daily deviations are then selected by deviantART and 'official' volunteers to create presentations for the homepage. These processes provide a way for artists to have their work recognised, and be promoted by the community.

Traditionally, artists produce works that gain attention through exhibitions or the forwarding by arbiters of taste like curators, gallery owners or art buyers. Exhibition curators are responsible for selecting the works that are to be presented at exhibitions, and thus act as the arbiters of what is and is not considered art, or at least what is considered high culture, worthy of display at a gallery or in an exhibition, and what is considered low culture.

Online art sites like deviantART provide new ways for artists and amateur artists to present their work and have it judged by other users, rather than by the arts establishment alone. Furthermore, as Salah (2010) points out, if we judge museums and galleries in terms of visitor numbers to their websites, we find that deviantART has a much more significant web presence than some of the leading cultural institutions, including the Museum of Modern Art, the Metropolitan Museum of Art, the Louvre and the Tate.

What is striking about this function of deviantART is that in providing a platform for artists to gain recognition, it is providing a role that is very similar to that traditionally provided by galleries. The major difference here is that all works are potentially visible, and the selection of works that are presented is a function of community selection, rather than selection by an expert such as an exhibition curator. SNSs like deviantART therefore raise questions not only about the status of the artist, but also about the institutions that make choices about what is and is not considered art.

Dan Perkel argues in his dissertation 'Making art, creating infrastructure: deviantART and the production of the web' (2012) that Web 2.0 isn't creating new forms of art or artistic practices, but rather the fabric of the web is a 'multi-faceted form of infrastructure' that forces old tensions in art to collide with Web 2.0 ideals. This then, in turn, produces new tensions. Reflecting upon the changing nature of IP and art theft, Perkel considers 'two commonplace notions: (1) that a new generation of Internet savvy creators are upending old ideals about art as property and (2) that the Internet is a medium for sharing rather than control' (2012). This leads Perkel to conclude that as well as creating new tensions between sharing and theft, there is a new balance between sharing and control. Far from disrupting '[r]omantic conceptions of art and creativity', Perkel argues that the web uneasily accommodates these multiple and often conflicting ideologies (2012: 1).

VERNACULAR CREATIVITY

If amateur art questions the boundaries of art, then vernacular creativity stretches them even further. As we have seen, websites like deviantART support communities of people who create and share creative works. Outside of arts-focused SNSs like deviantART is a world of ordinary, everyday creative production. This everyday creativity includes a range of creative activities that are rarely commercialised and which are very unlikely ever to appear in museums. It includes things such as travel photographs, family photographs, photo album arrangement, needle stitch, quilting and so on – all often practical or instrumental pursuits, but also undeniably creative.

Jean Burgess (2007) has called this kind of creativity 'vernacular creativity', drawing upon the word 'vernacular', which implies language that is ordinary and everyday. This kind of creativity clearly predates modern technologies by hundreds if not thousands of years, but the rise of social media means that these forms of everyday, ordinary creativity can be circulated and shared. Furthermore, the growing ubiquity of devices like mobile cameras and the creative potential of modern computers for video and digital art have meant that there has been an explosion in the production of vernacular works.

A good example of this kind of everyday vernacular creativity is the photographic vernacular, which refers to images of the everyday and banal that started to appear, as photography became more accessible to a mass market. Photography moved out of the realm of the professional and into the amateur and domestic. This was brought about by the development of Eastman's Kodak camera. As Burgess discusses, the Kodak camera made photography an everyday activity by making it available to everybody. Vernacular photography emerged as people began to take images in the course of everyday life, capturing glimpses into the personal and private. Travel and holiday photos, family photos and a miscellaneous array of images of people, animals, architecture and anything else that took a person's fancy soon began to become commonplace.

If the Kodak camera made photography an everyday activity, then the digital camera has democratised the technology, and the advent of the internet and photo-sharing websites such as Flickr has pushed this even further. The emergence of the digital camera, especially with its ubiquitous appearance on mobile phones, suggests a democratisation of media. Those who previously couldn't afford cameras or film processing costs suddenly have access to cheap and convenient alternatives, which has opened up the world of photography to people who would formerly have not had the time, technical knowledge and/or money. For example, in Seoul, the ready availability of digital cameras has seen some women develop a love of photography that has sometimes ultimately led to them wanting to become professional photographers (Lee 2005). We discuss some of the key emerging visualities around camera-phone images in social and locative media spaces in Chapter 7.

However, for Burgess, the term 'vernacular creativity' embraces two important concepts: the everyday or ordinary, but also a concept of *situated* creativity, because vernacular also implies locality and context dependence. Burgess cites Batchen (2001), who describes a range of ways in which people used photographic prints: arrangement in photo albums, as grids hung on the wall with an implied narrative, using photographs in ornaments, and using photos or parts of photos in scrapbooking. Thus, when a photographic print is placed into an album, it is done so in relation to other objects and the structure and affordances of the book form itself. To take a photograph out of an album, to find it isolated from its original context, changes its meaning.

Although vernacular creativity operates outside the purview of art, it should not be seen as 'other' to art. Burgess argues that rather than moving away from art practices and mass culture, vernacular creativity often engages with it, reproducing, mimicking and borrowing techniques. This means that at the boundary there is often no clear distinction between vernacular creativity and art: 'the boundaries between vernacular creativity and art or commercial mass media are, in practice, consistently permeable and transitory' (Burgess 2007: 35).

However, while the vernacular may not be the opposite of art, it is traditionally placed outside the sphere of art. With the exception of recent moves to embrace social histories, galleries and museums have traditionally ignored the vernacular altogether. Stallabrass points out that unless a vernacular object is extremely old, it is not acknowledged by art history, galleries or museums:

> Whole categories of visual cultural production never gain art-historical attention – amateur photography is an example, along with a large swathe of online practices, including the vast majority of the photographs uploaded to Flickr. (2010: 5).

Ignoring everyday creative practices belies their importance. The kinds of questions that are being raised are those we have been engaging with throughout this chapter: what is the nature of the division between the amateur and the professional, and who is the arbiter of what should and should not be considered art?

Context has important ramifications in online and digital media, too. Ito and Daisuke Okabe (2005) made this point clearly in examining the three Ss – sharing, storing and saving – of camera-phone usage. Taken out of context, the vernacular photograph from the mobile phone may seem banal, even narcissistic, depending on the content. However, in the social context for which they were developed these photos take on other meanings, just as if they had been arranged in a photo album. This contextualised sharing of images is not just about creative practice, but also a part of broader media literacy and etiquette (Koskela 2004). Within SNSs like Flickr (Mørk Petersen 2008) or deviantART, the social matrix established by the SNS and the people using it provide context. Comments, friend lists, watchers, favourites and a range of other site-specific tools all work together to contextualise the image and give it specific local meanings within a community. This dynamic environment in which strangers and intimates are sharing images and comments (both aesthetic and technical) suggest that new visualities are ordered by a 'situated creativity' (Burgess 2008) and also new geosocial cartographies (Hjorth and Gu 2012).

As camera phones become more commonplace with the explosion of smartphones – along with new contexts for image distribution like micro-blogging and location-based services (LBSs) – we are witnessing emergent types of visuality. In particular, through LBSs such as Facebook Places, we see ways in which users create new contexts for the overlay between place, ambient images and geographic locations. While, globally, camera-phone genres like self-portraiture have blossomed, we are also witnessing the flourishing of vernacular visualities that reflect a localised notion of place-, social- and identity-making practices (Lee, D-H 2009; Hjorth and Gu 2012). We discuss this in greater detail in Chapter 7.

CONCLUSION

This chapter has looked at the impact of social media on art as a way of examining the broader questions about the emerging relationships between social media and cultural production. As we saw at the beginning of the chapter, cultural production has come to be understood as something that involves the consumer as well as the producer. Social media invites new modes of cultural production where the user pays an even more active role by actually producing cultural objects rather than just interpreting them. The result of this is not only that more people can now produce and disseminate culture, but also that institutions and individuals who have traditionally been a part of this production process are having to adapt to these new modes of production.

This can be seen in the way that cultural institutions – galleries and museums – have begun to focus more heavily on their audiences. While there are other factors in play that are only tangentially related to the evolution of the internet, social networks have nonetheless provided a way for museums and galleries to engage with audiences. Consequently, we are now seeing people being included in cultural processes that were once solely the domain of curators and other experts.

For artists, the response to social media has been more mixed. Some artists, like Man Bartlett, have engaged with social media, working it into their artistic practice. However, as artists engage with social media and the internet, they also raise questions about the nature of the artist and his or her relationship with their audience. Other artists and art collectives, such as the Candy Factory, prefer not to see themselves as social media or internet artists at all, but are instead artists who use the internet. For other artists still, such as Cao Fei, social media and the internet open up spaces for critical analysis that engages with audiences and again complicates the role of the artist and his or her audience.

The complexities that these artists are grappling with belie the still-dominant concept of the artist as a member of a privileged elite. However, as we saw in the example of deviantART, art and cultural production is not the domain only of those with the 'right' background, but increasingly it is becoming the domain of people who produce creative works but whose work would rarely be considered by the art establishment. Instead, sites like Flickr and deviantART are providing alternative forums for the presentation and critical assessment of creative works and promoting works based on community consensus.

This trend is exacerbated by the increasingly important and visible role of everyday creativity in which vernacular forms of cultural production, such as mobile-phone imaging, have become part of the structure of social networks. While not new, vernacular creativity is revealed within social media as playing an important role in mediating social relationships. It does this through contextually nuanced performances that often engage with and adopt the codes and themes of both popular media and art.

In the final analysis, it seems clear that the shifts we have identified in other chapters, from mass audience to individual user, and from customisation to personalisation, are also being felt in the sphere of cultural production. These changes promise to have significant implications not just for how we conceptualise and understand art, but also for a whole range of creative practices and their role in society more generally.

6 Social media games

Social media games are games that are played within social network sites (SNSs). These games, with names like Happy Farm and Mafia Wars, are a familiar and integral part of using SNSs for many people. They are both a source of entertainment and a way to maintain relationships with friends and family. Thus, for people who study social media, social media games become an important part of the overall experience of social media, and demand attention. For games-studies scholars, the emergence of social media games (which are generally termed 'casual games' within the industry) is also significant. Social media games are being played by people with different motivations and different demographics than those who play games on consoles or those who play conventional computer games, and they are presenting a new economics of game production, which has seen new players enter the market. For some, like Juul (2009), the emergence of social media games constitutes a 'gamification' of culture, a casual revolution.

In this chapter, we are going to examine the emergence of social media games from both a social media and a game-studies perspective. In the first part of this chapter we look at the idea that games are social, which is at odds with the popular image of computer games in Western culture. Following this we consider social media games more specifically, paying particular attention to their role within social networking sites and identifying some of the unique features of these games and the associated implications for gaming and social media more broadly. As part of this analysis we look at the way in which social media games provide socially valuable spaces, but also acknowledge that these spaces are not provided for purely altruistic reasons; behind the games are SNS and games companies that rely on social gaming as an important source of revenue. The final part of this chapter presents a case study that brings the conceptual ideas we have discussed in the chapter together. The case study focuses on the uses of social media games in China and the way that the games are mediating relationships between generations as young people are increasingly moving away from their home and families for study and work.

FROM GAMES TO CASUAL GAMES

In the past, computer games have stereotypically been portrayed by the media in Western cultures as solitary activities for children who are socially inept and/or physically moribund. However, the growth of the computer game industry in recent years has made these ideas about games difficult to maintain. Furthermore, with the rise of so-called 'casual' games, more and more people are playing a wider variety of games, often in new and unconventional ways. In this section we will look at the evidence that games are not only social, but can also play a broader role in our social interactions generally. We begin by examining the social nature of games before looking at the rise of casual games as specific examples of the changing nature of the games industry. This will provide us with the background for the second section that will look more specifically at social media games.

Games and the Social

Despite having received a reputation as a solitary and socially isolating pursuit, games have in fact long been associated with conviviality (Salen and Zimmerman 2003). For evidence of this, one only needs to think of games that require two or more players (think of chess, backgammon, bridge, poker, mahjong, Monopoly, Twister) to notice that games that are played solo (solitaire, patience) are the exception rather than the rule. While many computer games are designed for a single-player experience, even here there is a great deal of social activity that extends from the game but may not be immediately apparent (online discussion forums, for example), to say nothing of the many, many games which are played as multiplayer games in an online environment (Taylor 2006).

Recent interest in massively multiplayer online games (MMOGs), fuelled by the success of games like Activision/Blizzard's World of Warcraft, is just the latest engagement between academic scholars, games and sociality (Corneliussen and Rettberg 2008; Nardi 2010). Some of the earliest research into online communities focused on text-based multi-user games called multi-user dungeons/domains (MUDs). Numerous scholars such as TL Taylor used these early multiplayer gaming environments as exemplars of online sociality. For example, Curtis (1996) examined the scope for social interaction afforded by the online environment while Reid (1995) argued that MUDs produced communities and forms of rich online sociality.

More recently, Steinkuehler and Williams (2006) have argued that MMOGs provide a rewarding and engaging online social environment. The authors conducted two extensive studies into MMOGs (Lineage and Asheron's Call) in which they interviewed participants and played the games, taking notes and recording the way that other players were engaging with the game. In one of the studies, the researchers found a sample of 750 people who did not play the game Asheron's Call; they gave copies of the game to one half of the group, and used the other group as a control. Using these methodologies, the researchers were able to gain some insights into the way that people socialised on MMOGs and on the differences between playing and not playing. The results of the two studies were convergent (they came to the same conclusions), both agreeing that MMOGs represented a significant social environment. For Steinkuehler and Williams, people's use of MMOGs had a social dimension that fits within Oldenburg's concept of a 'third place' (the social space beyond work and home, discussed further in Chapter 2). The studies provide further tangible evidence of the social nature of games.

Beyond the games themselves, gaming has been a source of sociality as players build forums to discuss games and develop user created content that ranges from fan fiction to game 'mods' that see players become creators and actively hack games in order to customise them. Far from being an isolating or solitary experience, game-playing is often a highly social experience, especially when games move into online multiplayer environments. If games can be social, then it might also be fair to say that games are frequently found alongside social activities, and in this respect SNSs are certainly no exception. SNS-based games are extremely popular, as we will see below, and have played an important role in building the subscription bases of social media as players seek friends to play with.

Yet games have often been disconnected from other forms of analysis because they are frequently conceptualised, especially in Western culture, as something that exists outside of everyday life, in a kind of sealed-off space of their own. This idea of games as being separated from other social activities reflects early debates about cyberspace as a place that is different from the offline (we touched on some of these arguments back in Chapter 2). However, as the internet grew, it became apparent that the exceptionalism that dominated early writings about the internet hid the fact that the same inequalities that existed offline were duplicated online (Nakamura 2002). And, as we saw in Chapter 3, there is also strong evidence to suggest that offline relationships have a very important bearing on online relationships amongst users of SNSs.

In the literature on games, the idea that games are separate to other parts of life was explored as far back as 1938 by Johann Huizinga, who examined games in his book *Homo Ludens* (1938 [1970]). Huizinga was fascinated by play and wanted to understand its function in culture. One of the concepts described by Huizinga in his book was the idea of the 'magic circle', a concept that was picked up and popularised by Katie Salen and Eric Zimmerman in their 2003 book *Rules of Play*. For Huizinga, Salen and Zimmerman, the magic circle acted as a site for play that was separate and removed from the real world. Inside the magic circle was the game world which was associated with play rather than reality. Thus inside the game world you are completely free to play, to try things out and to fail without fear of there being any real-world repercussions. There is no sense that the barrier between the game world and the real world is at all permeable.

Thomas Malaby offers a useful counter position in which he critiques what he sees as the exceptionalism in much game and play scholarship that continues to separate play from everyday activity (2007). One of the critical points that Malaby makes here is the idea that play can be usefully thought of as a mode of experiencing reality, rather than a separate activity that has no bearing on the real world. For Malaby, games are a set of processes that are linked to experience; many non-game activities have playful elements, just as many games have strong relationships with the real world. Using examples of both digital and non-digital games, Malaby provides empirical evidence to show that play is not always separate, safe or necessarily pleasurable, and that these notions of play are culturally nuanced and socially constructed. He also suggests that the division of work and play into separate spheres of experience may be a cultural artefact, rather than a universal distinction. Here Malaby points to work by scholars like Sherry Ortner, who defines the distinction between work and play/leisure as a 'modernist affectation' that results from the nineteenth-century construction of the idea of work (Malaby 2007: 8).

Astute readers will already have noted the parallels between the idea of the magic circle and early constructions of cyberspace in internet theory. Both have been seen as separate places that are disconnected from the real world. Yet, just as internet theorists have come to see the importance of the offline in the online, so too game theorists have begun to question this rigid separation of games and other aspects of social life. These insights into the position of games with respect to the other human activities become more important as we consider social media games which, like SNSs, are sites for social activities and where online and playful activities intersect with the social. As we will see below, social media games play an important role in SNSs, helping to recruit new users, and also providing a way for SNS users to maintain and develop contacts with their friend networks. Before delving into social games, however, we need to contextualise the development of social media games within the broader phenomenon of casual games.

Casual games

Casual games, as the name suggests, are games that can be enjoyably played without the high level of attention that is associated with non-casual games. These are games that do not require the same investment of time, and so appeal to a broader market than traditional console or PC-based games. The games are typically said to be easy to learn (but perhaps difficult to master). However, as Juul (2009) points out, these stereotypical definitions of casual games often do not withstand close scrutiny.

Many social media games fall into the general category of casual games by virtue of their design and their mode of play. While many social media games are casual games, it is not true to say that all casual games are social media games (many casual games are designed to be played on smartphones or other mobile devices, and often have little if any integration with social networks). However, to understand the role and importance of social media games, it is useful to understand them in the broader context of casual games.

As noted above, possibly the most distinctive feature of casual games is their light-attention mode of engagement, or their 'interruptibility' as Juul terms it (2009). Where traditional computer games encourage players to set aside hours for dedicated play, and reward players accordingly, casual games allow players to engage with the games for minutes at a time, dipping in and out of the game as time and interest permit. This different mode of engagement has a number of significant implications for game producers. First, casual games appeal to a broader range of people who do not have the time or inclination to play games that require them to put aside hours of dedicated playing time. Second, this low-attention mode of play means that casual games are well suited to environments in which the user is likely to be engaged in more than one task. For example, casual games are well suited to mobile devices, where players can play the games during brief periods of leisure throughout the day: during lunch breaks, waiting in a queue, or even while they are working, switching between work tasks and social media as time permits. For some, social media games allow people to be present in two social places at once, ushering in forms of 'presence bleed' (Gregg 2011) whereby boundaries between work and leisure blur.

Casual games also provide different incentives for play. As Hou (2011) points out, games designed for dedicated play focus on mastery of difficult tasks, demand full attention, and punish players for failure. For example, MMOGs have traditionally been the preoccupation of 'hardcore' gamers, demanding full attention and the investment of many hours of continuous gameplay. In MMOGs like World of Warcraft, failure at tasks is often treated harshly (with the death of a character and a penalty extracted in loss of accrued experience), and players who do not spend hours obtaining the correct in-game equipment find they cannot participate in activities with other more committed players.

By contrast, casual games present players with easier challenges and reward players for succeeding, sometimes excessively. This different dynamic makes casual games easier for a more casual gamer to engage with, and makes them less likely to leave the game out of frustration. This view of casual games as being gentler with the player is not universal, however. While Juul accepts that rewards are handed out frequently in casual games (a feature Juul refers to as 'juiciness'), he also argues that casual games do punish users for failure, but that 'you rarely fail due to a single mistake but rather an accumulation of mistakes' (Juul 2009: 42). This maintains a pressure on the player to succeed, but reduces the penalty for failure. For example, in FarmVille (one of the biggest social media games) crops can wither and die, and weeds will come to take over a farm if the player leaves it too long, but no matter how bad it gets, it is always recoverable. The key point here is that casual games are more forgiving than traditional games.

For the games industry, casual games have opened up a new and lucrative market that includes new, vastly increased numbers of players and a more diverse demographic. Demographic groups that have traditionally been difficult for the games industry to reach (people over the age of 40, and women, for example) are engaging with casual games. Many casual games seem to cross cultural boundaries, with leading games enjoying huge levels of popularity in many countries. Even MMOGs have now become casualised (Juul 2009) and part of the daily diet of many millions of SNS users. For many players, the importance of these casual social games sometimes eclipses the SNS itself. This new market for games has seen a number of formerly small game development companies like Rovio (Angry Birds), Zynga (FarmVille) and PopCap Games (Bejeweled) grow into multi-milliondollar companies by focusing their development efforts on casual games. Recognising the emergence of this market, larger game companies like Electronic Arts are now making games for the casual market and are also reaping the rewards.

Why have casual games emerged now, and what is driving their uptake? From a technical vantage point, the capability for mobile phones and web browsers to support casual games has been available for many years. Casual games have come of age now not so much because the technologies are available, but because there are now platforms that support the distribution of these games. To put it another way, although the technology to make casual games has been around for more than ten years, there was no consistent way for game developers to get their games to large groups of users and to receive suitable financial compensation in order to make casual game development an ongoing reality. Furthermore, the wide variety of different mobile technologies, each with their own nuances and technical limitations, meant that game development for the mobile market was extremely labour intensive.

For casual games on mobile devices, the important market development has been the emergence of smartphones, which are unified by their operating systems and associated app stores (the big names at the time of writing are Apple iOS, Google Android, RIM BlackBerry and Microsoft Windows Mobile). These operating systems, along with their online stores, provide a means for game developers to produce a game for a single platform (rather than a hundred different phones) and, significantly, to distribute the game within a system that allows them to profit from each game sold. For many game developers (especially smaller companies), the royalties that can be garnered from selling a game through an app store are significantly higher than would normally flow back to them if the game were published in a traditional retail outlet.

Web-based casual games have also come of age as the platforms to support them have developed. Again, the technical capacity for web browsers to support games has been around for a long time. A key technology is a software application from Adobe Inc. called Flash. Flash is a tool that allows the production of interactive content that can be delivered via a web page, and for many years Flash provided the only consistent way to develop and distribute web-based games. Many games have been developed, and advertising supported web gaming sites like Newgrounds, FlashPortal and Kongregate encourage Flash game developers to upload their games to the sites. These Flash games are often supported by advertising, which is facilitated by the sites (with game makers getting a royalty based on how popular their games are), or on in-game advertising, which also sees royalties flow to games based upon a variety of metrics.

Social media games

If the enabling development for mobile casual games was the smartphone and the associated app stores, then the equivalent for web-based casual game developers has been the SNS. It is here, at the intersection between casual games and social media, that we see the emergence of the social media game.

SNSs like Facebook and MySpace provide a platform for game developers that offers added benefits for the developer, in much the same way that app stores and operating systems offer benefits for mobile game developers. By developing a casual game for Facebook, for example, a developer can gain access to the user's friends' lists and add a social dimension to the game. This allows successful game developers to access many more people than if their game was placed on a standard Flash game site, thus increasing the total number of players, which in turn translates to a more profitable game. To illustrate the relationship between SNSs and game developers, we will examine the relationship between two of the largest – Facebook and Zynga.

There has been a lot of interest in social media games, driven partly by the popularity of SNSs, but also because the success of some social media games has demonstrated that these games can be just as profitable (and in some cases, more so) than console or PC-based games. The two factors that feed into this are the lower cost of developing a social media game, and the potentially broader audience of users that the game will attract. One of the major game production companies, Electronic Arts, acknowledged this when they purchased the UK-based social game development company Playfish for US$300 million in 2009 (Playfish 2009).

SNS-based games can collect revenue from advertising, from in-game purchases or from promotional marketing (Shin and Shin 2011: 854). In-game purchases are small payments made by players as they play a game to enhance their utility within that game. For example, a player who is playing Happy Farm can use real money to purchase virtual goods, such as seeds for the farm or decorations. To a non-player, the idea of spending money on virtual goods may seem ridiculous, but this kind of purchasing represents an important source of revenue for companies like Zynga, who have said that they derive 90 per cent of their revenue through in-game purchases of virtual goods. To illustrate the kind of money involved here, consider that in July 2012 Zynga reported that they had 306 million players per month and revenue from these users of US$332.5 million, of which US$291.5 million (close to 90 per cent) came from online games, the remaining amount coming from advertising. So, game and in-game purchases make up the bulk of Zynga's income, and although Zynga also sells games directly on mobile platforms, revenue from Facebook games continues to make up the lion's share of Zynga's profits (Zynga 2012).

While the SNS provides a valuable platform for social media games, it would be a mistake to think that the relationship between SNSs and social media games is one-way. Symbiosis would be a more accurate characterisation of the relationship between SNSs and SNS-based games. There are a number of reasons for this. SNS games are a method of recruiting new users to the SNS. Many games reward players with game bonuses, in-game gifts and/or currency for recruiting friends. For the committed player, the incentive to get all their friends and acquaintances involved in the game is significant. Once a player has exhausted their online friends, there is an incentive to get even more people involved by encouraging friends and family to join the SNS. Beyond the recruitment of new users, and perhaps more significantly for established SNSs with already large user bases, games also provide a revenue stream.

The importance of the game revenue stream is highlighted by the symbiotic relationship that has developed between Zynga and Facebook. Zynga, as mentioned above, is one of the most successful SNS game developers. In 2011 when Facebook made its initial public offering (meaning it would list on the stock market so people could buy shares in it), it revealed that Zynga accounted for 12 per cent of Facebook's revenue (Geron 2012). Zynga and Facebook had entered into a five-year partnership in 2010 in which Facebook guaranteed Zynga a steady increase in the number of users, and Zynga guaranteed Facebook that it would make its web games exclusively for Facebook.

Another indication of the importance of games (and Facebook apps generally) for Facebook can be seen in the deployment of Facebook Credits. Facebook Credits is a system designed to allow Facebook users to pay for content within Facebook. The idea is that you use a payment system, like a credit card or PayPal, to buy Facebook credits. Then, if you're playing a game like FarmVille, instead of paying for in-game purchases with your credit card, you use some of your Facebook credits. This system has one major advantage for Facebook: it allows Facebook to take a cut of all in-game purchases. The amount that Facebook takes is 30 per cent, so if someone buys a virtual chicken coop for US$3.00, the game-maker gets US$2.10 and Facebook gets 90 cents. Multiply this by every transaction on Facebook and it can add up to a lot of money. Even if Facebook decides to phase this system out, it will probably continue some kind of 'pay by Facebook' scheme, where users can opt to make online payments with a Facebook account rather than a credit card.

While the examples we have presented here have focused on Facebook and Zynga, they are provided here only as examples to illustrate the kind of business that is going on behind the scenes of social media games. In the future perhaps neither of these companies will exist, having ridden a wave of investor enthusiasm that ended up being little more than another dot-com-style bubble. They might both exist in a different form; the future is a dangerous thing to predict. The key point to take from this is that the strategies that underlie Facebook and Zynga's approach to the online environment are representative of the business of social media games. From the above, it is fair to say that to Facebook and Zynga, the value of social media games is that they provide another way for SNSs to commodify users' sociality. As discussed in Chapter 3, SNSs are businesses, and thus need to make money. They do this by deriving profit from their users, primarily though analysis of user's submitted data, and selling highly targeted consumers to advertisers. Here, SNS games provide a kind of platform-within-a-platform for deriving profit from the sociality of online games.

To this point, we have focused on the economic aspects of social media games. This is important because it outlines the environment in which social media games exist. Understanding the economics of social media games gives us important insights into how the games are designed. For example, once we know that the major source of revenue for Zynga is the purchase of virtual goods, it becomes clear that the economic imperative for the designers of the game is to make virtual goods a central design feature of the game.

PLAYERS AND SOCIAL MEDIA GAMES

While understanding the economics of the social media game is an important part of understanding the games themselves, it is only part of the picture because it tells us what game designers are trying to achieve with social media games, which is not necessarily what is actually happening online. To get closer to completing the picture of social media games, we also need to examine how and why people actually use social media games, and what they get out of them.

Given the revenue that successful social media games have made, it is perhaps not surprising that there are numerous studies that attempt to define what makes a social media game successful in order to come up with a formula, or at least a series of guidelines, for social media game developers. Shin and Shin (2011), for example, suggest from their preliminary research that people are more likely to play a social media game if they perceive it as playful. This might seem obvious at first glance, but motivations for playing games can be quite varied. Other studies have suggested that players are motivated to play games for reasons such as the thrill of competition and the satisfaction that can be gained from beating the game. In their study, Shin and Shin are suggesting that the capacity for playful behaviour within the game (that is, a game that allows players to interact beyond a set narrative of the game) is more important in SNS-based games than in other online games.

The importance of playfulness in social media games is also echoed by Kirman (2010), who emphasises the importance of what he calls 'gaps' in game design. These are the places in which there is space for the players to deviate from the game's overall design. These gaps allow players to experiment playfully with the game and to come up with new and unintended (from the designer's perspective) ways of playing games. This can range from players of a game like FarmVille creating designs and illustrations by planting their crops in strategic positions (something that the game supports, but was not designed to do), to players subverting the intended success or winning conditions of the game. Kirman cautions against social media game designers becoming too formulaic, suggesting instead that leaving gaps in the design of the games is a desirable thing that can have positive, if unpredictable, side effects. In essence, the more latitude the players have to experiment within the game, the more playful the game and the more potential it has to become successful.

Studies that have looked at the demographic profile of social media gamers have tended to suggest that when compared to players of conventional games on consoles and PCs, social media gamers are generally older, more likely to be female and do not necessarily identify themselves as 'gamers' (ISG 2010). We do need to approach these claims with some caution, as much of the research has been conducted by the industry, who have long desired to see games elevated into a more mainstream pastime. The study methodology is a little opaque (it is not clear how the sample was selected), and the study does not actually define what they counted as a social game. However, the notion that casual games appeal to a broader section of the community than so-called 'hardcore' games seems a reasonable assumption that is supported by the research, and if we are to take the statistics at face value we might also wonder if the motivations that people have for playing these games have also changed.

An important source of the research into social interaction in online games has come from research into MMOGs. These games boast large user populations who are often deeply engaged in social activities within the game environment. For example, Yee conducted a study of 30,000 players across a number of MMOGs and found that primary motivating factors for people to play MMOGs were social interaction and achievement, noting that 'MMORPGs [massively multiplayer online role-playing game] attract a diverse demographic who are drawn to the environment to socialise and interact with other users' (2006: 320). Williams et al. (2006) conducted a study that looked closely at social structures called 'guilds' in the World of Warcraft MMOG and found that for many players the MMOG was a space that acted to support existing online relationships. In other words, people who knew each other socially offline would use MMOGs as a convenient place to socialise online. These findings are similar to studies of users of SNSs that we discussed in Chapter 3, who also seem to socialise primarily with people they know in an offline context.

Yet while the research into MMOGs gives us some insights into the ways that people use games as social environments, the research into MMOGs does not necessarily always translate to social media games. MMOGs such as Everquest and World of Warcraft are games that are hardly casual. In fact, these games are often associated with time-consuming attention-demanding play that rewards players for time investment and, in the case of World of Warcraft at least, virtually requires that players form groups at higher levels to continue playing the game and progressing. Casual games, by comparison, do not demand the same kind of time investment, and so it seems reasonable to hypothesise that a different level of engagement would yield different kinds of social interaction. It is also possible that games that are designed to operate within an SNS provide different environments which may influence the way people socialise within them.

One approach that begins to develop insights into these questions compares games that are designed to work within an SNS with stand-alone games to determine what (if any) effect social networking has upon the structure of games. Kirman et al. (2009) conducted one such study and have suggested that one of the reasons for the popularity and rapid growth of SNS games when compared to stand-alone games is because of the intimate nature of the game request. For a stand-alone game to pick up new players, it needs to recommend itself either through advertising or word of mouth. For social games on SNSs, the word-of-mouth method becomes very powerful not only because it is easy, but also because the recommendation to play the game inevitably comes from someone in your social network. In other words, if a good friend invites you to play a game with them you are more likely to say yes.

Other studies have analysed the social networks constructed by social media games, or have asked questions of the players directly. In her study of social media games, Hou (2011) found that players do not seem to be motivated by challenge and competition to the same degree that players of conventional games are, but instead play social media games for relaxation and diversion. This, she suggested, reflects the casual nature of social media games. Specifically, they do not require extreme expenditure of time or attention and do not punish failure. Importantly, however, Hou also found that the social dimension of social media games was important for players. According to Hou, 'respondents played social games more frequently, spent more time on the game, and got more engaged in game activities for the purpose of social interaction' (Hou 2011). Hou's research suggested that social interaction was the most significant reason for playing social media games. This is somewhat at odds with the ISG (2010) report mentioned above which found that only around 25 per cent of their respondents identified social interaction as the major reason for playing social media games. Respondents to that study nominated relaxation and enjoyment as their primary motivation.

It is not clear why there is a disparity between the ISG study and Hou's, but the methods used for analysis, including the way in which the respondents were selected, may play a role. One of the key issues here is that there is a tendency in some research to generalise the player population. Players are not one homogeneous group, but are diverse, and different people play different games in different ways. Not all players of social media games approach them with the same casual attitude, and some social media games promote different kinds of game play than others. Some players do invest serious amounts of time and resources in social media games, and could be termed 'hardcore' players, even though they play casual games. Referring again to the ISG (2010) report, 12 per cent of US and UK social media game players play their games for more than ten hours a week, and 9 per cent play social media games for more than three hours at a sitting. It is reasonable to hypothesise that the experience and motivations of social media games for these hardcore players is somewhat different to the average player who, according to the ISG report, plays social media games for one to five hours a week. The more hardcore players can also have a stronger influence on the game than more casual players. That is, a small number of players can be responsible for a very large proportion of interactions within a game (Kirman et al. 2009). These players, while in a minority, may be responsible for a disproportionate amount of apparent social activity within the game.

If we consider that different players may play social media games differently, then it is just as important to consider how different kinds of social media games can affect player sociality. Rossi (2009) suggests that social media games can be grouped into two broad categories based upon how the user's friend network is utilised by the game's design. The first type is 'skill/ knowledge' games, which essentially challenge the player to accomplish a given task or answer a question. In these games, SNS friends are fellow competitors, to be played against and/or ranked against in a score table. The second kind of social media game identified by Rossi are managerial or, as Rossi terms them, 'truly social' games, in which the object of the game is not to win so much as to build and develop a virtual space populated with virtual goods. This would include games such as Happy Farm, FarmVille and Pet Society. In these games, the goal is to maintain and perhaps develop your virtual space through regular maintenance.

These different kinds of game would tend to suggest different modes of play and different ways to involve friends. The skill/knowledge games require more attention over shorter periods of time (depending on the game). Friends in these games are competitors, and are more likely to be drawn from a closer group of people you know, people with whom you have strong ties in a social network. Truly social games are played over long periods, often having no defined end-point or winning strategy, and require the user to dip in for relatively short periods to perform basic maintenance tasks. Friends in these games take on a new dimension as the game rewards players with virtual goods for recruiting new players and sharing or helping out other players. In these games, friends become game resources where the more friends you have connected with, the more agency you have in-game. Even with such broad categories of social media games, and rough/confusing delineations of users into 'casual' and 'hardcore', it becomes clear that there is no one way to play social media games, and that the levels and kinds of social interaction are going to vary from user to user and game to game.

It is perhaps not surprising that some have argued that social media games may not be as social as they may seem. While a game like Happy Farm appears ostensibly to be a hot-bed of social activity as users increase the size of their social networks, more often than not this behaviour is purely instrumental. As Shin and Shin put it, '[i]n social games friends are not really friends, they are mere resources' (2011: 853). In other words, the game rewards players for inviting new players, and so players comply, but this does not necessarily lead to those players going on to be sociable in that environment. For Rossi (2009) this then leads to the idea that there can be at least two kinds of friends in an SNS gamer's network: real friends (that is, people who they socialise with), and instrumental friends (who are on the user's friend list within the SNS, but who might otherwise have only a very weak relationship with that user).

This raises an important point about sociality within the social media game. The game can act as a kind of catalyst for other social behaviours, and may spawn further kinds of sociality and creative production from players. Rao (2008) has previously argued that social games are inherently social, and may constitute a third place for sociality (in much the same way that Steinkuehler and Williams argued that MMOGs construct a third place). For Rao, social media games can foster relationships by providing a forum for socialisation that is separated from the mainstream way that this is performed in an SNS. An example might be a mother and daughter who play an online game together regularly. The game provides a scene for online sociability that probably would not have existed in the user's conventional SNS activities, which is reserved for other kinds of (non-family) contact.

The remainder of this chapter is dedicated to a case study that examines some ways that social media games are played in China. In this case study Happy Farm (an adaptation of FarmVille) features prominently, although other games are also mentioned. Many of the themes discussed above are played out in the case study, demonstrating that social media games do play an important and sometimes surprising role in online social interaction.

In particular, the case study provides qualitative insights into how social media games are being used socially to bridge social gaps that have opened up in a country that is experiencing rapid development and social change. This serves two purposes. First, it highlights how some of the conceptual ideas about social media games work in practice; and second, it demonstrates that social media games are not just Anglophonic phenomena, and are not just used by the young.

HOME AND AWAY: A CASE STUDY OF SOCIAL GAMES IN CHINA

> Cultures ... [do] not hold still for their portraits. (Clifford and Marcus 1986: 10)

The rise of social games such as Happy Farm, played through SNSs such as Renren and Kaixin, have seen millions of people young and old participating in their communities of practice. According to iResearch, a consulting group specialising in internet research, around 50 per cent of the 26 million daily users of one of the main SNSs, renren.com, play online games (Cheng 2010). These games generate around half of the website's annual income. Whilst the number of traditional network games (like MMOGs) has remained relatively constant at 50 million, SNS users have burgeoned from nothing to tens of millions in a few years (Cheng 2010). This phenomenon, whilst highly social, also demonstrates changing attitudes to both the online world and gaming.

The success of Happy Farm in China may have something to do with the context of Chinese society more generally (Hjorth and Arnold 2012). China is going through a process of rapid development and industrialisation and is transitioning from a communist to a capitalist economy. The communist underpinnings of Chinese society are still very much a part of the educational system, and all educated Chinese children graduate from school with a firm understanding of Marxist and Maoist philosophy. Happy Farm allows people to play with the basic economic model of capitalism, replete with the morally questionable practices of theft to increase one's personal wealth. In addition to this socio-economic backdrop, rapidly increasing real-estate prices in major population centres like Shanghai and Beijing means that for many, the thought of owning one's own home is an elusive dream. Against this backdrop Happy Farm is a nostalgic fantasy that rewards hard work (represented in the game by hours online) with a successful farm.

Happy Farm is in many ways the epitome of the casual social game, and the central game mechanic is a simplified model of capitalism. The object of the game is to start with a very basic farm with few resources and to develop the farm over time by acquiring, raising and selling produce for a profit. One of the key – albeit subversive – factors of this game is to steal other people's produce when they are offline. While this is a slightly damning condemnation of the morals (or lack thereof) of capitalism, it serves an important function for the game in keeping players engaged.

Many Happy Farm players keep the game open on their desktop whilst doing other activities (such as work) to avoid being robbed. Some have been known to set their alarms for late in the night so they can go online when everyone is asleep in order to steal. Interaction with friends is built into the mechanics of the game through a number of features. Players can gain experience points by helping their friends develop their farms, and are rewarded with in-game gifts (that help players improve their farms) for encouraging their friends to play the game. Hou (2011), although acknowledging the limitations of her study and warning against generalising her results, found that the elements of social interaction in Happy Farm encouraged people to play the games more frequently for longer and with higher levels of engagement.

While the casual game connotes a less attention-intensive mode of gameplay, it would be wrong to think that this translates to less engagement. Unlike their 'hardcore' predecessors, SNS games are much more casual in their demands for engagement. However, behind this casualness is a play architecture that is often just as time-consuming – but just in the form of distracted micro-engagement. Users often have the game open on their desktop behind other screens like word documents, email, instant messaging and so on whilst their virtual plants mature and grow. Leave the vegetables too long and they will wither and rot, and weeds will grow, so the pace of the game is slower and requires less intense attention than hardcore games, but it still requires attention.

Interestingly, the demographic of players migrating to these games don't consist of the obvious demographic of the young student. Instead, it seems that the fastest growing demographic is parents and even grandparents. They are often being taught how to use the internet by their children, who are living away from home for study or work. This cross-generational new media literacy emerging in China's increasingly mobile population (that is, migrating to cities like Shanghai for work or study) sees social media such as QQ (the largest and longest-running SNS in China) and online games as helping to alleviate the negative effects of cross-generational class mobility by maintaining kinship relations.

In China, the generation of children born in the post-1980s period are called the *ba ling hou* (literally, the 'after 1980s': *ba ling* is 1980 and *hou* is after). The term has been used in a similar way and with similar connotations to the use of the Anglophonic term 'generation Y'. Children from the *ba ling hou* generation grew up in a rapidly modernising, post-cultural revolution, one-child family China. As a result, these children are characterised as spoiled and self-centred but also technologically adept and more open-minded than older generations. Reflecting the rapid urbanisation of China, many people from this generation move to find work or take up study in urban centres, so it's not unusual to find *ba ling hou* living away from their familial support structures. Like all generational generalisations, of course, the idea of the *ba ling hou* is more an embodiment of social anxieties and hopes about the present and the future than it is an accurate description of real people, so we can see that the characterisation of the *ba ling hou* represents a generation at the forefront of significant social and economic change in China.

Interviews with young adult users of Chinese social games provides us with some valuable and surprising insights into the ways that the issues surrounding the uses of social games and inter-generational politics are being played out in China. In a study conducted by Hjorth and Arnold (2012), they saw that it was a desire to maintain inter-generational connection as students left home for work or study that encouraged communication via social media and especially social media games.

Maintaining these relationships requires work that, for a time-poor student, was sometimes regarded as laborious. For example, one female respondent aged 25 played online games such as mahjong (an online version of the traditional Chinese board game) because her mother liked to play them with her. She said, 'The more I play, the happier my mother is. I like to make her happy.' Another female respondent aged 20 complained that she believed her father to be addicted to playing games. She said, 'He has so much time on his hands, he just wastes it on gaming. Our generation don't have time.' This is an interesting role reversal in the stereotypes associated with age and media practice. Rather than children being accused of wasting their time with new media, instead parents are often called out for excessive online media use.

Another female respondent (aged 19) said her parents were still learning to play games and use social media like QQ. Her parents were retired and they now had time for the student to teach them new media skills. This education was not always a great success:

> They have a lot of time to stay at home, so they will play the computer games and want to surf online. But my father and mother are not good at it yet, so I continue to teach them and with the help of QQ, I can contact them more often. For example, when I come back home, I find that my father's mobile phone has something wrong – it always happens and he can't receive my short

message. I said he's a little old for it. He has played games in QQ and also, Happy Farm. He liked stealing vegetables. But my uncle is more of a social media user. Several years ago, we taught him how to use the internet – how to connect and talk with others by QQ or something like that. *And now he uses it all the time.* He even makes friends with strangers. And so, every time I come back to my home and we can talk a lot about QQ and games. I don't know if the technology is a very good thing for him. I don't know, because I think maybe he has spent a lot of time on this new technology, maybe too much. Personally, I have no doubt he has a very, very young heart from his technology use. And I think he is enjoying his life very much. (Hjorth and Arnold 2012)

This respondent invested time and energy in getting her family online and bringing them up to a level where she could include them in the social activities, like playing Happy Farm. While her parents seemed to be slow in the uptake of the technology, her uncle took to it with alacrity, which the respondent found a little surprising. Like the previous respondent who disapproved of the amount of time her father spent online, this respondent disapproved of her uncle's use and noted with great surprise how willing her uncle seemed to play with strangers online. She viewed her uncle's attitude as demonstrative of a type of youth or youthful attitude, or what could be dubbed a type of 'kidults' (adults adopting kid-type attitudes to lifestyle objects like new media). Here we see that knowledge of new media is equated with a type of youthfulness, but not knowing the often-tacit limits of media practice seemed to be the *faux pas* for older users (according to *ba ling hou* respondents).

Another respondent, this time a 23-year-old female, also indicated that there was effort required to maintain these social connections, effort that was sometimes more than she was willing to expend. This respondent liked playing a variety of games that reflected two worlds – the casual and the hardcore. She liked both casual games like Happy Farm and hardcore games like World of Warcraft. However, she found that she has too many friends on her SNS, Renren, which means that once she starts playing one game she gets caught up and finds it hard to leave and get work done. So now she mainly plays the online game on the local university server. As she notes:

I liked playing Happy Farm very much. I think the plants I planted are very beautiful and I like to keep my farm looking neat. I also like visiting other people's farms and stealing some plants and flowers from friends. Often I'm playing in the same [physical] space as my friends. It adds to the enjoyment of the game ... I think it is very good for socialising, but then I became too busy and it was hard for me to stop playing when friends were logging on. I now use a local game developed at Fudan University. It is good because I just play that one with my friends and roommates at the university. We play when we have all finished or need a break studying. (Hjorth and Arnold 2012)

For her, playing online social games is a social activity, and one that's sometimes carried out with her friends in the same physical space. But the intensity of this activity became too much, and began impinging upon other aspects of her life, so she moved her activities into another space where she has less social connections to maintain. For this respondent, the labour associated with maintaining too many connections was too great to justify continuing to play the game.

For the *ba ling hou*, social games are not only about play, they are also about the work of maintaining relationships. This is a full-time intimate labour that requires effort for the user to maintain. Like playbour (forms of labour carried out in and around computer games), and the work that modders (those who modify games' software) do, this labour is essential to the economics of social games and social network sites. As Kücklich's (2005) example of the modder illustrates, the modder has to call upon their various forms of labour (social, creative, affective, emotional) that reflect their community and the associated modes of knowledge. This process is an integral part of the gaming communities – a labour of love that is supported and then turned into profit by the industry (Andrejevic 2011). Media such as SNSs and social games can be seen to operate to exploit a type of full-time intimacy in which work and life boundaries continue to blur (Wacjman et al. 2009).

In this case study we have seen how SNS games amplify the local. Through the case study of Chinese social media games we see the growing tensions around forms of socio-economic mobility for the *ba ling hou* as they try to be both at home and away; a process in which intimacies are negotiated across private and public, work and life spheres. The constant contact afforded by social and mobile media means that users can be operating across various forms of co-presence. In SNS games like Happy Farm, we see new forms of cross-generational media practices that are indicative, and symptomatic, of China's transformations.

CONCLUSION

Games are social activities, and it is no accident that some of the earliest as a well as some of the most current forms of online sociality take place within the framework of games. While there is a tendency to regard games as something that is separate to real life, games must, as Malaby (2007) points out, be understood as a mode of experiencing reality, one that is no less valid than other modes. So, when we come to look at social media, it is hard to ignore the great degree to which games have found their niche. As we have seen, social games – as games that are played within the constructs of SNSs – have attracted great numbers of players, brought new subscribers to SNS sites and have opened up both gaming and social media to demographics that were not otherwise engaged with them.

Social games are social because of the fundamental role that social engagement plays in them. All social games, in some way or another, utilise people's friends, or the potential for people to make new connections in the online environment. This makes these games more enjoyable, and provides playful ways for people to socialise in online environments. Playing social games requires players to engage with the game in different ways that are often more socially oriented, and thus embedded in offline contexts. This, in turn, has given birth to new forms of player practices. These games are no longer about hardcore, subcultural practice, but are casual, in that they require less intensive attention than hardcore games – they are interruptible (Juul 2009) – and have various mechanics that make them appeal to broader audiences.

This is not to say that all social media games are the same, or that all players interact with these games in the same way. While some users play social media games competitively with their friends, others tend virtual gardens for hours a week, this time accumulated from many small moments snatched throughout the day. Some only play games with friends, and others play games with family as a way to maintain contact. Still others collect SNS friends (who may not be actual friends, but friends only as defined by the SNS) as resources that give them greater utility within their virtual space. The uses of social media games are almost as varied as the people who use them, but as we saw in the case study, there are familiar motivations even across language and cultural boundaries. Social media games are playing a central role in the ways that people socialise within SNSs.

7 Social, locative and mobile media

While Hyunjin waited for Soohyun in a café in Shinchon, South Korea, she toyed with her iPhone. Having downloaded some of the numerous photo apps, she began to experiment. Finally she was happy with the Hipstamatic lens that made her coffee look like it was out of some old analogue photo shoot. She then quickly uploaded it, along with the caption 'Waiting', to a few social media sites with location-based services (LBSs) like Facebook Places and Cyworld *mini-hompy*. While the relevance of the caption might be lost on many of her friends, for Soohyun it served as a reminder that she was keeping her friend waiting as she dashed from the train station. Another friend of Hyunjin, Joon, was in the area when she saw her friend's photo message and her location via her phone. She quickly made a detour to the café and sneaked up behind Hyunjin. Both girls laughed and shared a coffee while Soohyun raced to get to the café in busy peak hour traffic.

Toshi had never understood why people used the LBS game *Foursquare* until after the earthquake, tsunami and nuclear disaster of March 2011 in Tohoku (called '3/11'). During 3/11 he tried in vain to make contact with his parents, finally making contact hours later and after much distress. Access to social network sites like Mixi was difficult with mobile phone (*keitai*) networks jamming. Moreover, with loss of electricity, Toshi found himself in an unfamiliar situation – no working *keitai*. So when some sort of normality was established after 3/11, Toshi began to constantly use Foursquare not to play the game but as a way to give his friends and family a way to always know where he was.

Over in Shanghai, a mother, Jia, misses her daughter, Yuewen, who has just moved away for university work placement. Thoughtfully, before she left, Yuewen installed the most up-to-date software on her mum's pirated smart-phone (*shanzhai*). As instructed by her mum, Yuewen installed all the most popular games, especially social media games like the farm simulation Happy Farm, for even though the game had its heyday in 2009 it is still played by millions today. So Jia logs onto China's version of Facebook, Renren, and signs onto Happy Farm. She sees Yuewen is not online and so not protecting her crops. So Jia uses the most popular instant messaging (IM) service, QQ, to send a message to Yuewen to see if she has time for a quick play in Happy Farm. For Yuewen, typical of China's Generation Y (*ba ling hou*), LBS mobile games like Jiepang, along with microblog Weibo, are her favourite media. However, when she reads her mum's message, she quickly signs into Happy Farm to reconnect and catch up on gossip with her mum.

Grandmother Amy had never been a technology kind of person. She grew up in an age when technology was a male domain. On the other hand, her husband was a passionate adopter of new technologies and always had the newest Apple Mac item on hand. But one day, Amy's husband brought home an iPad with some of her favourite books uploaded. The next minute, Amy was hooked. Before long she had numerous games and social media apps downloaded, thanks to her enthusiastic grandchildren. Before long, Amy, like so many grandparents in Melbourne, had joined Facebook. And with that membership, her relationship with her grandchildren took on new forms of intimacy. While Amy was a little unsure about the ways in which her grandchildren seemed to impulsively upload pictures and make comments, she enjoyed seeing this other side to them and their friends – their 'mobile publics' if you will.

As a mother of two adult children, Penelope had begun to reacquaint herself with new media. The first thing she did was buy an iPhone. After a decade of using one of the first generation 'classic' Nokias, which was only capable of SMS and voice calls, Penelope's world quickly expanded. Having never used Facebook prior to the iPhone purchase, Penelope was quick to adopt new social and even locative media practices. She loved catching up with old friends overseas that she hadn't seen for decades. It created a new world of possibilities and conversations. But her children weren't so keen. Once upon time, Facebook was their social media world. Now, people over 55 are the fastest growing users of Facebook in Australia (SEO Sydney Blog 2009), and parents and grandparents seemed to be dominating the space. So Penelope's children and their friends, like many others, responded to their parent's online presence by changing their privacy settings and defining their online boundaries.

These examples are but a few of the millions of intimate vignettes that describe the ways in which mobile social media is being deployed. Across numerous technical platforms, personal and cultural contexts, and through a wide variety of social media, people young and old are using social, locative and mobile media to rehearse earlier forms of ritual and, at the same time, create new forms of intimacy and different contexts for the expression of intimacy. While locations like Seoul and Tokyo have long been centres of innovation in the invention and popularisation of mobile media, the relationship between personal, social, locative and mobile media is quotidian and, for the most part, tacit in its familiarity. In other locations like Australia or the US, convergence in the form of smartphones is nascent. Mobile social media is a global phenomenon, but also local at every point (Hjorth and Arnold 2013).

Having explored the convergence of social network sites and games in the last chapter, this chapter looks at the way in which mobile media has increasingly become the key portal for social and locative media as smartphones increasingly, and unevenly, are adopted around the world. Devices such as the iPhone have become synonymous with this media evolution. Through this growth, we have witnessed a shift from the device being analysed as communication medium to being understood as a networked media tool in which social media, games and various forms of everyday creativity can be found (Hjorth et al. 2012). In the short few decades in which mobile phones have been readily available, this technology has changed from being a mere extension of the landline to being a sophisticated and convergent online mobile media portal (Goggin and Hjorth 2009). For many, mobile media is the key device and context for online and social media, with locations like Japan having more than a decade of mainstream mobile internet. In China, three-quarters of its 485 million online users (318 million) access the internet via mobile media (CNNIC 2011). In locations like Singapore and Melbourne (Australia), the rapid adoption of smartphones has seen a rise in cross-generational social media usage – much to the disgust of some younger users who fear their parents won't understand much of the tacit etiquette.

Over the few decades of mobile phone use, the analysis of mobile communication has rapidly expanded to encompass many disciplinary and interdisciplinary approaches such as sociology, anthropology, internet studies, games studies and new media studies. While not everyone has a computer, the ubiquity of mobile phones in places like China and India have provided many with access to a version of the online. But while mobile media is a global phenomenon, it is also reflective of the local at every level. The growth in mobile media has served to amplify the various complex dimensions of locality, rather than eroding the importance of place. This interdisciplinary context has afforded the study of mobile communication a rich history of mixed methods and conceptual paradigms. But it also means that studying mobile communication has become the battleground for some of the various disciplines' boundaries.

All over the globe, location-based services such as the global positioning system (GPS), geotagging and Google Maps have become a pervasive part of everyday life through platforms and devices such as smartphones, Android devices, tablets and portable gaming devices. Moving beyond printed maps, mobile digital devices now frame and mediate our ability to traverse, experience, share and conceptualise place. This shift appears to have a range of consequences for our relationships to place, intimacy, privacy, time and presence. Locative media shapes, and is shaped by, a variety of factors such as culture, age and temporal differences.

In this chapter we reflect upon the journey of the mobile phone as it has unevenly developed into social, locative and mobile media. In particular we look at the development of LBSs, often integrated with social media, that have converged with mobile technologies in the smartphone. Acknowledging the increasing use of these converged devices, we look at how mobility has become about more than the ability to take your social media with you.

Specifically, there are two results of media mobility: the expansion of cartographies enabled by LBS devices and mobile apps, and the development of location-based social apps that blend social relationships with geography. These changes reflect broader shifts in the relationships between identity, place and community and raise important issues about privacy, but also how we narrate and attach meaning to place. In the next section we reflect upon the nature of the convergence of mobile, social and locative media. This is then followed by a discussion of the changing role that camera phones play in our understandings and visualisations of place, especially as they become entangled in locative media practices.

MOBILE, SOCIAL AND LOCATIVE

Over a short few decades, the mobile phone has expanded from being little more than an extension of the landline into this century's version of the Swiss Army knife (Boyd, J. 2005). In order to encompass this transition from a mere communication tool to a multimedia device, the rubric of 'mobile media' has been deployed (Goggin and Hjorth 2009). Currently the hottest must-have consumer device is the smartphone, a general term used to describe mobile devices that can access the internet and support a range of applications (apps) that can be downloaded and installed by the device's user. Smartphones also boast a range of ways of sensing their environment, from GPS to digital compasses and tilt-sensitive accelerometers. Smartphones have brought a new dimension to social media as their 'always on' internet connectivity, combined with their support for a wide range of applications, means that people can now engage with social media anywhere, anytime.

The 'always on' nature of mobile media is amplified in the case of smartphones. These devices can be viewed as a kind of identity caravan, in that they mobilise, tether and contain the user's inner world and their sense of home (Hjorth 2012). Smartphones work as both a portal for new media and as a remediation of older media practices, such as television via YouTube. The concept of remediation was first used by Bolter and Grusin (1999) to describe the dynamic and interdependent relationship between new and old technologies. Far from old media being superseded by new technologies, a cyclic relationship ensues. An example can be found in analogue and digital photography whereby rather than the digital erasing the importance of the analogue, much of the digital is in fact haunted by the analogue. Digital software programs such as Final Cut and Photoshop reference the analogue in the ways in which their editing techniques are named and structured. Camera-phone apps such as Hipstamatic increasingly deploy the analogue look for a retro aesthetic. Mobile media is a great example of remediated media; it houses many media and apps that are a hybrid of new and old media. Along with housing remediation, mobile media also operates as a vehicle for 'presence bleed' – a term Gregg uses to describe the bleeding of one's personal presence across platforms, contexts and media (2011). We have previously examined this term in Chapter 6 as a part of our discussion of the 'always on' nature of social media and casual games.

Along with the changes in the technology have come changes in the profile of the people who use the technology. Associations of the mobile phone with ostentatious wealth that accompanied the first generation of mobile phones in the Anglophonic world are now almost completely forgotten as cheap phones are plentiful and coverage is wide, even on a global scale. While for many of the world's poor countries, mobile phones are 2G (second generation, that is, non-internet), according to the International Telecommunication Union (ITU) (ITU 2011), this is rapidly changing as markets for pirated smartphones have seen phenomenal growth. Some statistics suggest that as of March 2012 China's mobile phone subscriptions topped 1 billion (CNNIC 2012).

The increasing use of mobile technologies worldwide is also seeing the growth in the use of mobile internet, which is enabled in part through the increased accessibility of smartphones. With prices being driven down by demand and competition in some of the most populous countries in the world, smartphones are becoming increasingly accessible even in developing countries. Cheap smartphones and *shanzhai* (imitations of brand-name phones like Apple's iPhone) are now readily available, and prices keep falling as companies develop low-cost phones for the burgeoning markets of China and India.

Until recently in many countries – especially the Anglophonic world – the evolution of the mobile phone has appeared in the form of a transition from a mobile communication technology to a mobile multimedia technology. But, as social media becomes mobile, it is also beginning to converge with other technologies, such as LBSs, that continue to redefine the uses of the mobile device. LBSs utilise various features in smartphones (including GPS, and various methods of triangulating position based on proximity to cell-phone towers and wireless networks) in order to determine the location of the user in geographic space. LBSs in current smartphones allow the phone to determine its position to an accuracy of within 100 metres, usually much less.

Although LBSs have been available in mobile devices since the early 1990s, it is only fairly recently that LBSs have become a feature of smartphones, and so have started to become available to people who would not otherwise have gone out to purchase a separate device such as a GPS unit. While locative media, like the Internet, has its history in the military, GPS was quickly adapted for commercial use. However, locative-based mobile games were developed from an experimental and creative context (de Souza e Silva and Hjorth 2009) that has later taken the form of commercial games such as Foursquare.

The transition of LBSs can be thought of in terms of generations. The first generation of LBSs were available through custom devices which provided a single-use device, often seen in countries such as the US and Australia only in higher-end motor vehicles. The use of first-generation LBSs saw some innovative experiments with play, but was constrained largely to experimental uses by early adopters. Second-generation LBSs have emerged as GPS and GPS-like services that are embedded in consumer devices as just one of many features on those devices. With the more general accessibility of LBSs, the experimental uses of the technology have been commodified and are moving beyond gaming and into other applications. The most immediate impact of these second-generation LBSs for users of smartphones is through services like Google Maps, where an interactive map can pinpoint a user's location and calculate the fastest route to almost any destination. Although the navigational capabilities this affords are important, the feature only represents a fraction of the implications of LBSs, particularly when they converge with networked media. It should also be noted that while this convergence of mobile, locative and social media is quite new in some countries (particularly in the Anglophonic world), in other countries, like Japan, the mobile phone (*keitai*) has been associated with social and locative media for over a decade (Hjorth 2003; Ito 2005). Now, with the increasingly widespread use of smartphones and the convergence of mobile, social and locative technologies in these devices, the implications of convergence are being seen in many places.

For obvious reasons, place has always played an important role in mobile media (Ito 2002; Hjorth 2005), but the ramifications of these changes go beyond the immediate promise of being able to access the internet and social media anywhere, anytime, or of mapping one's position in the world (as useful as that may be). Mobile media highlights the various, often-tacit notions of place as something that is lived and imagined, psychological and geographic (Hjorth 2012). As mobile media converges with social and locative technologies, new forms and practices are emerging that are especially focused on developing social connections. These technologies can be seen as increasingly overlaying space with digital information in order to create new *places* that are mediated in part by the technology itself. These new places are not entirely online, since they are fundamentally rooted in geographic space, but neither are they entirely offline – they sit somewhere in between.

These 'hybrid' spaces, as Adriana de Souza e Silva calls them, create social situations in which borders between remote and contiguous contexts no longer can be clearly defined (Gordon and de Souza e Silva 2011: 86). Instead of us understanding our world in terms like online and offline or virtual and physical, we are increasingly engaging with a reality in which the physical and virtual are merged to some degree. These spaces are not just mediated in this way, but can also become localised; that is, a hybrid reality places us and our social connections at the centre of not just our social world (as we discussed in Chapter 3), but also at the centre of our understanding of the hybrid physical world. Buildings, parks, pubs and churches become enhanced with meanings that are associated with them by us and our friends.

As these hybrid realities emerge, new cartographies also emerge. Here we use the term 'cartography' to refer to the practice of making maps, though not necessarily visual ones. Maps function as representations of the world, allowing us to navigate to what we are looking for by helping us to orientate ourselves in our environment. They are abstractions of the real world, as they only show the things that the map-maker feels are important. Nautical maps indicate water depths, while land maps indicate the location and size of roads. Maps link space with place, where place is the concept of a space that has meaning ascribed to it. As noted earlier, although place has always mattered to mobile media, this is magnified in the case of locative media. Later in this chapter, we will reflect upon how locative media and camera-phone practices are shaping, and being shaped by, our conceptions of place and locality. But first, let us try to untangle one of the most shifting notions being redefined by social, locative and mobile media: place.

RETHINKING PLACE: IMAGES OF GEOSOCIAL MAPS

The contestation of the term 'place' is further magnified through mobile media. Increasingly, urban spaces are being mediated by technologies. Mobile media not only mediates intimate relations; it also mediate how we experience and think about spaces and places. Place is not only a space with geographic contours, it is a space that operates across many levels: imagined and lived, social and physical. While nineteenth-century narrations of the urban were symbolised by the visual wanderer of the *flâneur*, the twenty-first-century wanderer of the informational city has been rendered into what Robert Luke calls the 'phoneur' (2006). The *flâneur* was both a voyeur and part of the urban spectacle of the growing bourgeoisie: the phoneur sees the city transformed into an informational circuit in which the person is just a mere node with little agency.

The impact of networked and locational media on place cannot be underestimated (Farman 2011). Digital, mobile maps change how we navigate and conceptualise place. Consider how the act of looking up a journey via printed paper road maps is a distinctively different experience and conceptualisation of space when compared to the automated and digitally co-present experience of LBSs. LBS games like Foursquare and Jiepang highlight how place cannot be mapped just as a geographic or physical location, but also reflects cultural, emotional and psychological dimensions.

Through the convergence of social, locative and mobile media we are seeing the contested notion of place becoming even more complicated. Michel de Certeau famously defined place as a '"proper" and distinct location', whereas *'space is a practised place'* (1984: 117). This is a little confusing, because it is counter to the common-sensical way in which most people use these two words, in which space is merely a geographical location and place is a space invested with emotional meaning. In this chapter we, like many other cultural critics, will use the terms 'space' and 'place' in their colloquial sense. For example, Tim Cresswell defines place as 'a meaningful site that combines location, locale, and sense of place' (2009: 1), and Doreen Massey sees places as entanglements and combinations of the 'stories-so-far' (2005: 130).

While maps give us one sense of space, they are incomplete in conveying the complex and often competing cartographies of place. As Massey notes:

> One way of seeing 'places' is as on the surface of maps … But to escape from an imagination of space as surface is to abandon also that view of place. If space is rather a simultaneity of stories-so-far, then places are collections of those stories, articulations within the wider power-geometries of space. Their character will be a product of these intersections within that wider setting, and of what is made of them … And, too, of the non-meetings-up, the disconnections and the relations not established, the exclusions. All this contributes to the specificity of place. (2005: 130)

In Wilken and Goggin's timely *Mobile Technology and Place* (2012), the various authors reflect upon the conceptual currents and controversies facing notions of place in the face of increasingly ubiquitous mobile and location-aware devices. With the 'spatial turn' in media studies (Falkheimer and Jansson 2006), entanglements between space, mobility and sociality have, for good reason, been further complicated. For Wilken and Goggin:

> place is considered fundamental to the construction of our life histories and what it means to be human, while mobiles now form an intrinsic part of the

daily lives and habits of billions of people worldwide – and for the manifold ways that they mutually inform and shape each other. Place is a notion that is of enduring relevance – one worth mobilising – if we are to comprehend fully how we think about and experience who we are, where we are, and the ways we interact and relate with one another. In other words, place is considered a vital notion in that it represents a 'weaving together' of social and human-environment interaction in ways that situate place as central to how embodied, technologically mediated mobile social practice is understood. (2012: 18)

Locative social media such as Foursquare, SeeOn (Korea) and Jiepang (China) are fusing social media and LBSs through the mobile device, and often LBSs are being merged with other mobile device features – most notably camera phones. This media practice adds a great deal of complexity to the cartographies that are being constructed and shared by users. Personalised social maps are being overlaid on the geography, with personal recommendations about places to eat, or to stay away from, and even the location of friends mapped out through the mobile device, creating new ways in which place and co-presence is visualised, shared and memorialised (Hjorth et al. 2012). Ingrid Richardson (2011) argues that, through LBSs, mobile devices are realigning our experience of 'being online' by allowing us to reconceptualise earlier ideas which cast online and offline as binary opposites. This, in turn, opens up complex and dynamic ways of thinking about – and being – present.

In LBSs we see an overlaying of place with the social and personal whereby the electronic is superimposed onto the geographic in new ways. In particular, by sharing an image and comment about a place through LBSs, users can create different ways to experience and record journeys and, in turn, impact upon how place is memorialised. Although the area of locative media has attracted much critical and rigorous attention of late as a convergence between urban, gaming and mobile media studies (Gordon and de Souza e Silva 2011; de Souza e Silva and Frith 2012; Farman 2011), there are some gaps. Specifically, there is a need for case studies over temporal, cultural and generational contexts if we are to fully understand the impact of LBSs on relationships to people, place and privacy.

There are some key theorists who have really helped to forge this second generation of locative media studies as it moves increasingly into the mainstream through devices like smartphones. For de Souza e Silva and Daniel Sutko, net locality can be understood as the process whereby location-aware technologies create a perpetual, evolving dynamic between information as place and place as information (2009). While urban spaces have always been mediated by technologies, according to Gordon and de Souza e Silva net localities 'produce unique types of networked interactions and, by extension, new contexts for social cohesion' and so 'co-presence is not mutually opposed to networked interaction – and as emerging practices of technology develop, drawing the line in the sand becomes increasingly difficult' (2011: 91).

Through mobile media, the relationship between being online and being offline has shifted, creating new types of engagement and co-presence. Lines that mark out and differentiate the online and the offline, virtual and actual, here and there, are shifting and fading as these zones overlap, entangle and bleed into one another. It is in this context that Richardson and Wilken call for a post-phenomenological reading of body–technology relations in order to understand three key mobile media modalities: located presence, co-presence and telepresence (2012: 185). As both a disciplinary field and a movement in philosophy, phenomenology studies the structures of experience and consciousness from a first-person view. Key phenomenologists include Martin Heidegger, Edmund Husserl, Maurice Merleau-Ponty and Jean-Paul Sartre. Don Ihde has been categorised as a post-phenomenologist with his adapted version of phenomenology that encompassed the changes brought by technologies. For Richardson and Wilken, 'mobile media use occurs across a spectrum of "placing" and "presencing"' (2012: 185). They continue:

> Mobile devices clearly antagonize any notion of a disembodied telepresence that is seemingly endemic to digital screen media, as we are frequently on-the-move, on-the-street and purposefully situated in local spaces and places when engaged in mobile phone use and mobile gameplay. (Richardson and Wilken 2012: 184)

These authors argue that the 'meshing of located place and networked space' creates crucial questions, especially around whether mobile media 'collapse the space-place distinction, or enable "space" and "place" to be simultaneously present' (2012: 185). They argue that mobile media devices create a different dynamic around perpetually interrupted and distracted body–screen–place relations (2012: 194) in which 'placing' and 'presencing' are entangled. Building on Gordon and de Souza e Silva, Richardson and Wilken argue that mobile media practices involve a series of overlapping 'presences' (telepresence, co-presence, located presence and net-local presences) in everyday spaces (2012: 195).

These 'presences' and their intimate, social and networked affects construct a rich fabric of emotional, social, technological, electronic and geographic overlays that inform, and are formed by, existing social and cultural practices. To understand the implications of these presences on notions of place and intimacy, locative media needs to be studied as part of everyday social and mobile media practices. Case studies of educational, creative and experimental projects by researchers such as Gordon, de Souza e Silva and Christian Licoppe (2004; Licoppe and Inada 2006) are useful, but are limited because they are not studies of locative media in the context of the everyday. In particular, what has been missing from the conversation has been the role of camera phones in the use and adaptation of locative media in everyday contexts. As this chapter's opening vignettes described, with locative media there is more impetus for users to take and share camera-phone images as a place-making exercise that interweaves the social with the geographic. In the next section we consider the changing role of the camera phone as part of locative, social and mobile media networks.

THE PLACE OF IMAGES: LOCATIVE, SOCIAL MEDIA CAMERA-PHONE PRACTICES

While camera-phone genres such as self-portraiture have blossomed on a global scale, vernacular visualities that reflect a localised notion of place, sociality and identity-making practices (Hjorth 2007; Lee 2009) are also flourishing. Smartphone apps like Hipstamatic and Instagram have made taking and sharing photographs easier and more interesting. With LBSs like Facebook Places, Foursquare and Jiepang, we see a further overlaying of place with the social and personal, whereby the electronic is superimposed onto the geographic in new ways. Specifically, by sharing an image and comment about a place through LBSs, users can create different ways to experience and record journeys and, in turn, create an impact upon how place is recorded, experienced and thus remembered. This is especially the case with the overlaying of ambient images within moving narratives of place as afforded by LBSs. An example might be someone uploading a geotagged camera-phone image onto Facebook Places whereby the information of place is recorded and shared in a variety of ways. This practice, in turn, impacts upon their experience of place as something that is mediated through networked media. While place and intimacy have always been mediated by language, memories and gestures, it is the way in which they are being mediated that is transforming how we think about and practice place.

The rapid uptake of smartphones has enabled new forms of distribution and has provided an overabundance of apps, filters and lenses to help users create 'unique' and artistic camera-phone images. Although the iPhone has been quick to capitalise on this phenomenon through applications such as Hipstamatic, other operating systems like Android have also had their share of this expanding market. So too social media such as microblogs and

LBSs have acknowledged the growing power of camera-phone photography, not only by affording easy uploading and sharing of the vernacular (Burgess 2008), but also by providing filters and lenses in order to further enhance the 'professional' and 'artistic' dimensions of the photographic experience (Mørk Petersen 2008). Consider, for example, how social media applications for smartphones no longer ask you to go through multiple steps to attach images to a post. Formerly, if you wanted to post an image, you'd take the image using the phone's camera application, which would store the image in the camera's library, which you would then access by attaching the image to a post. Sometimes you would even need to upload the image to an online image repository so it could be linked to the SNS. Now, many social media apps provide a photo button integrated into the app that allows you to take a picture and post it immediately, and social media companies provide their own image-hosting servers that operate almost invisibly to the user.

CAMERA PHONE IMAGES: NETWORKED VERSUS EMPLACED

When visuality becomes part of a networked culture, its meanings, contexts and content change. Camera phones, as an extension of the networked nature of mobile media, are clearly defined by this dynamic. Although initial studies into camera-phone visuality discussed it as part of networked media (Ito and Okabe 2005; Rubinstein and Sluis 2008; Villi 2013), this second generation of visuality – one that is characterised by locative media – is about new types of place-making exercises. These exercises are emotional and electronic, geographic and social – highlighting the complexity of ever-evolving notions of place. In each location, camera-phone images are overlaid onto specific places in a way that reflects existing social and cultural intimate relations as well as being demonstrative of new types of what Pink calls 'emplaced' visuality, in which locative media emplace images within the entanglement of movement (2011).

First-generation 'networked' visuality, when combined with LBSs in the obvious case of the smartphone, becomes 'emplaced' visuality – that is, a visuality mapped by a moving, geospatial sociality (Pink 2011). Incorporating movement in the theorisation of visuality is important given the ways in which camera-phone practices give way to an accelerated taking, editing and sharing of a 'moment' that is then contextualised through its place in the moving geographic and social maps of LBSs and social media. Whereas first-generation camera-phone sharing was defined by the network (Ito and

Okabe 2006; Burgess 2007; Villi 2013), the second-generation, characterised by LBSs like geotagging, becomes focused upon emplacement through movement (Pink 2011). In other words, LBS camera-phone culture is about reinforcing the process of the node rather than the product of the network. Images increasingly become about creating a sense of movement through an ambience of place. These images are 'multisensorial' (Pink 2009) in that they evoke more than the visual; they overlay information (such as location) with emotion.

For Pink (2011), the combination of locative media with the photographic image requires a new paradigm that engages with the multisensoriality of images. It might at first seem odd to talk about images as being multisensorial, because surely images are visual, and so draw upon only one sense: vision. Pink draws on Tim Ingold's (2008) critique of the anthropology of the senses and of network theory as well in *Doing Sensory Ethnography* (Pink 2009), and argues that by exploring the visual in terms of multisensoriality one can re-prioritise the importance of movement and place.

For Pink, locative media provides new ways in which to frame images with the 'continuities of everyday movement, perceiving and meaning making' (2011: 4). By contrasting 'photographs as mapped points in a network' with 'photographs being outcomes of and inspirations within continuous lines that interweave their way through an environment – that is, in movement and as part of a configuration of place' (2011: 4–5), Pink argues that we must start to conceive of images as produced and consumed in movement. Here, we can think about how images are being transformed in the light of various turns: emotional, mobility and sensory. Indeed, of all the areas to be impacted and affected, camera phones – especially with their haptic (touch) screen interface and engagement, along with their locative media possibilities – can be seen as indicative of Pink's (2011) call for a multisensorial conceptualisation of images. As Pink notes, the particular way in which text, image and GPS are overlaid create a multisensorial depiction of a locality.

This shift can be viewed as the movement from a camera-phone visuality that is networked to camera-phone images which are 'emplaced' (Pink 2011). An image that is socially networked, tagged and GPS located is 'emplaced' in a number of ways. First, it is emplaced as one of many images captured by a particular member of our intimate or social public and is contextualised by our relation to that person. Second, the co-presence of many images arranged by time or place on the one site places each image in the context of others to constitute a narrative, and thus another context. Third, the GPS coordinates place the image in geographic space and invite the viewer to *recall* the place in question as well as *view* the image captured in the place in question, thus overlaying another context. Finally, the social distribution of the images creates a social public for those images, thus overlaying another context, and the image tags entered by the public overlay yet another context.

Devices and images

For Chesher (2012), the rise of smartphones like the Samsung Galaxy and the iPhone – with their attendant software applications like Instagram, Google Goggles and Hipstamatic – have created new ways in which to think about camera-phone practices and their engagement with both image and information. For Chesher, the iPhone universe of reference disrupts the genealogy of mass amateur photography. Chesher argues that up until camera phones, the Kodak moment dominated. This was then replaced by the Nokia moment, and then further colonised by the iPhone through the plethora of camera-phone apps available. Applications like Instagram which allow users to take, edit and share photos partake in what could be called a second generation of camera-phone and photo-sharing social media. With sites that allow the display of 'vernacular creativity' (Burgess 2008), Flickr being the precursor, Instagram heralds a new generation of visuality in which the cult of the amateur is further commercialised. Launched in October 2010, Instagram quickly grew to boasting over 150 million uploaded images. The virtual and viral nature of Instagram was illustrated by a graphic design firm in Italy who recently built a physical digital camera prototype that looks like the Instagram icon, called the Socialmatic. With these new applications, often working in collaboration with social and locative media, camera-phone images have been given new contexts.

For Daniel Palmer (2012), iPhone photography is distinctive in three ways. First, it creates an experience between touch and the image in what Palmer calls an 'embodied visual intimacy' (2012: 88). While 'touch has long been an important, but neglected, dimension in the history of photography ... the iPhone, held in the palm of the hand, reintroduces a visual intimacy to screen culture that is missing from the larger monitor screen' (2012: 88). Second, the proliferation of photo apps for the iPhone has meant that there are countless ways for taking, editing and sharing photos. No longer do camera-phone images have to look like the poorer cousin to the professional camera. Third, and most important to our discussion here, is the role of GPS capability with the iPhone automatically 'tagging photographs with their location, allowing images to be browsed and arranged geographically' (2012: 88).

As Palmer identifies, the placing of photos through tagging creates a different way of archiving and contextualising the image. With the growth in LBSs like Foursquare, Jiepang (China) and flags (South Korea) that allow users to 'check in' and upload pictures, networked visuality and the attendant empowerment/control binary is further complicated. For some, LBSs provide new forms of übersurveillance (Michael and Michael 2010) and stalking techniques (Gazzard 2011). For others, they highlight how the local continues to play a pivotal role in informing notions like privacy and sociality. LBSs allow already 'friendly' surveillance, such as that present in parent/child relationships, to flourish in new ways. In these new geospatial visualities, the motivations and types of genres are changing to reflect the ways in which locative media impact upon how localities are shared and experienced. Locality, gender and generation are all informing these visualities. In particular, the pivotal role camera phones have played in women's and girl's cultures cannot be ignored (Lee 2005; Hjorth 2007).

CONCLUSION

We began this chapter with an overview of the development of mobile technology, noting the development of LBSs and their integration into mobile media. An important point we made was that smartphones are emerging as converged technologies that bring together other technologies like wireless internet, LBSs, camera phones and so on. Mobile devices do not just extend the number of places that you can use social media; they bring social media to those places and, through the LBS, contribute to the construction of new cartographies of space. In other words, they provide us with new ways of mapping meaning to space and creating new places.

The growth of locative media is having significant impact upon cultural practice, place-making and relationships in ways that are shifting, ongoing and emergent (Cincotta et al. 2011; Farman 2011; Gordon and de Souza e Silva 2011; de Souza e Silva and Frith 2012). This phenomenon has both positive and negative impacts upon localised notions of privacy and surveillance across both micro and macro, and individual and collective, levels (Michael and Michael 2010; Gazzard 2011). While much analysis has been conducted into experimental forms of locative media/ art (de Souza e Silva and Sutko 2009; de Souza e Silva and Hjorth 2009), the increased ubiquity of locative media through devices such as the smartphone will undoubtedly transform the way in which place and mobility are articulated.

Although second-generation LBS games like *Foursquare* and *Jiepang* are in their infancy, they represent an area of growing diversity and complexity within mobile media and communication. In particular, LBSs are changing how we visualise intimate cartographies through shifting camera-phone practices. Whereas first-generation camera-phone practices noted gendered differences (Lee 2005; Hjorth 2007), through LBSs, these gendered differences in visualities take on new dimensions – particularly in terms of potential 'stalker' elements (Gazzard 2011; Cincotta et al. 2011). The mainstreaming of LBSs through smartphones is demonstrating the diverse ways in which privacy is understood across cultural, social, temporal and generational contexts. Future studies in locative media will need to reflect upon these issues.

8 Conclusion

Attempting to understand social media is a daunting task because the questions and problems that social media provoke are a reflection on some of the most fundamental questions we are grappling with in contemporary societies. As a vehicle for popular culture, social media is a dynamic and ever-evolving creature in which use-by dates perpetually loom in the face of the new, novelty practice. Consider Microsoft's Hotmail. Once the key email site, its use now evokes embarrassment and shame with comments like 'You're not *still* using Hotmail?' To use an old social network site (SNS) like MySpace evokes a reference to the user being not just old-fashioned but also obsolete. What technologies we use reflect our taste-cultures. They reflect localities as competing technological, socio-cultural, economic and linguistic spaces. Thus to understand social media, it is not enough to simply log in to Facebook and start participating; we have to look more deeply at the economic, political and social dimensions of the changes that seem to be associated with social media.

With any technology, especially one that seems to be so ubiquitous, it is tempting to fall into a technologically deterministic mindset. In other words, it is easy to see social media as a technology that is changing society. However, the relationship between technology and society is always complex, and social media is particularly so because it crosses through some of the most fundamental parts of our societies. Technology use is about cultural practice and, in this way, social media operates as a barometer of the politics of everyday life.

Rather than seeing social media as a radical technology that is changing society, in this book we have looked at social media from a number of different angles to examine the ways that social media is both changing society as well as responding to and *reflecting* changes in the society. This is a dialectic – a backwards-and-forwards discussion for the purposes of investigation – that ultimately determines what social media is and what it is becoming.

As we saw in Chapter 2, one of the fundamental issues is the tension between the empowerment offered by social media and the control and commercialisation that is seemingly interconnected. This tension is played out on numerous levels, and throughout the book we have returned to issues of empowerment and control as a recurring theme. In Chapter 3, for example, we looked at how the tensions between empowerment and control played out in SNSs. SNSs are empowering because they provide a platform that people can use to connect with each other, with numerous significant results. We looked at some of these results in Chapter 4 where we examined the practical implications of produsage as social media empowers users by making it possible for everyone to be both consumer and producer. The implications of this for journalism and social activism are only beginning to be felt. We saw similar questions raised in art practice and creative institutions in Chapter 5.

Our goal here has been to avoid reducing the empowerment/control dynamic to a binary. Polar opposites are useful for establishing the boundaries of a discussion, but in reality, nothing is ever entirely empowering, nor is it entirely controlling. A more productive discussion emerges when we understand that empowerment and control are tendencies in social media that raise questions which deserve careful consideration and exploration.

Another theme that can be represented as a binary is the relationship between offline and online modes of presence and co-presence. Here, we can go back to the early internet-studies literature and see the way that scholarship shifted from utopian or dystopian claims about 'cyberspace' to incorporate a more balanced understanding that articulates online experience with offline experience. When we come to examine the way people actually use social media, we find that studies and theorists again and again emphasise the importance of the offline in the online. In Chapter 7, for example, we looked at how locative media is converging with social and mobile media in ways that are shaping how we experience and conceptualise place. We also reflected upon the role camera phones play through geotagging and how this sharing of co-present visual ambience creates new ways for thinking about place and intimacy.

We have tried to maintain a global, or at least non-Anglophonic, perspective throughout the book. To understand social media increasingly implies understanding a technology that moves beyond the borders of the nation-state as it connects people across geographical boundaries, and in so doing structures our societies so that they resemble networks. As we saw in Chapter 3, networks have become an influential metaphor for understanding social structures in modern post-industrial societies. This can be a little confusing at first, because contemporary societies are networked in at least two ways: technologically and socially. Technologically, we are all aware that computers, coupled with electronic networks (most importantly, the internet) are a defining feature of modern societies, just as the steam engine and the factory were the defining features of industrial societies. However, when theorists like Manuel Castells (1996) declare that we live in a networked society, there is another subtle element being introduced. Here Castells is using the idea of the networked society as a metaphor for how the structures in society are being organised in a way that is similar to a computer network. For others, the analogy of the network seems to neglect the importance of the journey and movement within these spaces as part of broader entanglements of place (Pink 2011).

In Chapter 3 we examined some of the practical applications of this. Barry Wellman's notion of the networked individual represents a person who is able to control their social environment better because of their networked connections. People like boyd (2008, 2011) have argued that such networked-media forms as the SNS provide a place in which people can come together to form networked publics – publics that are mediated by the technology. To summarise boyd's argument as presented in Chapter 3, this mediation of the network plays an important role in defining what is different about these 'networked' publics. Networks extend the reach of publics geographically and temporally; for example, think of a special-interest internet forum. Members are from all over the world and while some might constantly monitor the forums, many log in just once a week. As boyd observes, 'as social networking sites and other genres of social media become increasingly widespread, the distinctions between networked publics and publics will become increasingly blurry' (2011: 55). In these dynamics, which some define as an intimate turn, the boundaries between social media and everyday life further erode.

While the networked qualities of networked publics are important, there is some evidence to suggest that something else is going on. As we saw in Chapter 3, studies in the US have found that people's online social networks often consisted of people who they knew well and who lived within a relatively small distance. Then, in Chapter 6, we looked at the way youth in China were using SNS games to stay in touch with their family as they moved away from home for work or study.

This brings us to a third central theme of the book: intimacy. Through their work looking at the uses of mobile and social technologies in the Asia-Pacific region, Hjorth and Arnold (2013) conclude that intimacy plays a very important role in social networking. They suggest the notion of 'intimate publics' to emphasise the role that intimacy plays in the construction of online publics. They are not arguing that networks do not also structure publics, but that intimacy is a primary structural factor. Intimacy here is not only romantic or familial intimacy, but also includes other kinds of intimacy, like the connection that two people have by virtue of the fact they went to the same school or come from the same country. As we have noted previously, as intimacy becomes increasingly public (Berlant 1998), we see various forms of 'presence bleed' (Gregg 2011) across publics, networks, SNSs, platforms and media. So too, the ways in which cultures are imagined and experienced rely on particular forms of cultural intimacies.

This movement of intimacy into the context of the social returns us to questions about empowerment and control. Instead, we can reframe the empowerment/control dialectic in terms of a shift in social dynamics in which displays of intimacy begin to play an increasingly important role in the way we socialise and interact with the media. For example, even jour-nalism has been affected by the intimacy turn through utilising an intimate mode of address online. As Goggin has pointed out, much of Twitter's eti-quette borrows from more intimate media like SMSs (Goggin 2011). This movement of intimacy into the public is not simply a phenomenon of social media, it is a social phenomenon that is shaping, and being shaped by, con-temporary media.

In the final analysis, then, we would like to think that *Understanding Social Media* is not about understanding the specific technologies and politics that are only associated with this month's stock market favourites. Far more importantly, *Understanding Social Media* is about comprehending the way in which this new medium is both affecting and reflecting social developments more broadly, and as a result of understanding social media, we will come to develop a better understanding of the world in which we live.

Glossary

API (application program[mable] interface) – a set of software tools that can be used by a computer programmer to access a complex web service or hardware component.

App – an application that is accessed by users over a network, or which is downloaded to a mobile device. The term is becoming complicated as the mobile 'app store' method of application delivery is extended to the desktop.

Big Data – the proliferation of data in current society.

Big Media – large companies that treat the news as a commodity, where costs of making news are pushed down while profits are maximised; this is rarely aligned with good journalism.

Casual games – social media games that allow players to engage with the games for minutes at a time, as opposed to the more demanding MMOGs.

Citizen journalists – amateurs offering an alternative to the mainstream media, operating mainly through their own blogs.

Clicktivism – the pollution of activism with the logic of consumerism.

Computational turn – a term that points to the way that computer technology appears to be changing processes and structures of existing organisations. For example, the computational turn in journalism relates to the way that news research and publication has been altered by the emergence of the networked computer and the internet.

Folksonomy – a portmanteau of 'folk' and 'taxonomy', meaning a classification system generated by the general public.

Gamification – making something more game-like by introducing game development principles into its design. An example might be educational software that aims to engage students by presenting educational material in the form of a game.

Geotagging – using an LBS (see below) to associate geographic location with some other kinds of data such as a photograph or text message.

GPS (global positioning system) – technologies that calculate the position of a ground-based device through satellite communication. Modern GPSs provide accuracy to within about 3 to 15 metres and are becoming a regular component in modern smartphones.

HTTP (HyperText Transfer Protocol) – the technical term given to the method for transferring web pages across the internet. Other internet services (like email) use different protocols.

ICT (information and communication technology) – a catch-all term that covers computer and network technology. The more pervasive ICT becomes, the less useful this term becomes.

IM (instant messaging) – a computer-based chat system that allows one or more people to 'talk' by typing words into the system. When the typed text is sent, the person or people connected to the chat session will see the other person's words instantly. This is similar to email in that it is text-based, but its speed allows for more rapid conversations to take place.

Intimacy – in common usage, this refers to very close relationships between people, typically lovers or family members. However, intimacies also exist when referring to social relations at larger scales. For example, there are intimacies between people who belong to the same country or culture (a large- or macro-scale social group).

ISP (internet service provider) – a company that provides a person or organisation with internet access, almost always in return for a fee.

Killer app – a software application that is so successful that it sells the platform that it runs on.

LBS (location based service) – a collection of technologies that allow a device to map its position. GPS is one LBS technology, but there are others, such as digital compasses, those that calculate a position by triangulating the signal strengths of known wireless internet or mobile signal towers, and those that use accelerometers in order to determine the orientation of a device with respect to the ground. Many LBSs use a combination of these technologies.

Local, the – a term that describes things that are close to an individual, not just physically (the local shops) but also culturally and socially (close friends, for example, may not be physically close).

Macro – cultural level.

Media – any technology that stands in between and facilitates communication between two or more people.

Meso – social level.

Micro – individual level.

MMOGs (massively multiplayer online games) – games that uses computer network technology (typically the internet) to allow many players to occupy a virtual game space at the same time such that they can interact with each other.

Mobile publics – associations between people (publics) that are made possible owing to or through the use of mobile technologies.

MSN (the Microsoft Network) – an early attempt by the software company Microsoft to create a proprietary internet-like online service.

MUDs (multi-user dungeons/domains) – like MMOGs (see above), but were text-based and descriptive instead of graphical.

Networked publics – public groupings that are structured by the logic and reality of computer networks.

OCR (optical character recognition) – a method for translating an image of printed text into letters and numbers that can be edited and searched on a computer.

Online activism – the use of internet or mobile (online) technologies to enhance, support and/or promote social activism around a topic or event.

Platform – a service or software application that supports other software or activities. For example, an SNS like Facebook is both a platform for social interaction and a platform for software apps such as Facebook games.

Produser – a user who produces (rather than just consuming) internet content. The term emphasises the highly interactive nature of much social media use, wherein the user often contributes their own creative products to websites. Produsage includes activities such as uploading videos and photos to web services like Flickr and building and maintaining blogs.

Remediation – a term used by Jay David Bolter and Richard Grusin (1999) to describe the way that new media tends to call upon the conventions of earlier forms of media. So, for example, photography remediates perspective painting, and YouTube remediates television.

Sentiment analysis – a technique whereby the computer attempts to determine the affective meaning of pieces of text.

Slacktivism – activism that is lazy, half-hearted and generally 'slack'.

Smart mobs – a large group of people who use mobile technologies as a way of connecting with each other, thus allowing the group to act with a kind of collective intelligence.

SMS (short messaging system) – the technical term for mobile phone texting; that is, sending short text messages from one mobile phone handset to another.

SNS (social network site) – websites that support or extend social networks. According to danah boyd, the basic requirements of an SNS are: 1) the ability to create a profile; 2) a 'friends' list or similar; 3) exploration of friends lists and perhaps others in the system (boyd and Ellison 2007). Typically, most online relationships are with people who are already part of the user's offline social network.

Social capital – once defined by Pierre Bourdieu (1984 [1979]) as social 'knowledge', the term has taken on a variety of definitions to reflect changing social relationships/connections and the fabric of community.

Social, the – a general term used to describe the social world that constantly surrounds us and in which we live. The term reminds us that although we live in a physical world of things, we also live in a social world, which has a very large influence on how we act and behave.

TCP/IP (Transmission Control Protocol/Internet Protocol) – the technical method that is used by computers to share information across the internet.

Ubiquitous computing – the idea that a computer can be accessed anywhere, anytime. The term has gained currency as computer technologies have become smaller and cheaper to the point where many people now carry around networked computers in their pockets in the form of a mobile telephone. Ubiquitous computing can also refer to the use of computers in objects like appliances and buildings.

UCC (user created content) – content that is created by non-professional people who would otherwise be considered consumers. Amateur photos, fan fiction and homemade video are all examples of user created content. In this book we prefer to use the term 'UCC' when we are specifically referring to works intentionally created by users.

UGC (user generated content) – this is similar to UCC but covers a broader range of user-produced material. In this book we define UGC as material that is produced as a by-product of another activity, possibly without any knowledge or intent on the part of the creator. An example of UGC could be forum posts, in which the content of the website is text created by users, and read by other users.

URL (uniform/universal resource locator) – this is a string of letters that describes where something is on the internet. A web site location, written like http://www.mysite.com is an example of a URL.

Vernacular creativity – this term was suggested by Jean Burgess (2007) in order to describe everyday creativity. This kind of creativity is distinguished from professional or artistic creativity because it is practised in non-work contexts and is designed for local consumption. For example, arranging and decorating a photo album is an act of vernacular creativity because it is in no way commercial, and the intended audience is local – friends and family. Vernacular creativity often has very situated meanings; in other words, the significance and meaning of pictures in the photo album can best be appreciated by close friends or family who share memories or knowledge of the people and places in the photos.

Web portals – sites that aim to aggregate users around centralised content.

References

Alden, C. (2005) 'Looking back on the crash', *The Guardian*, 10 March. Retrieved from http://technology.guardian.co.uk/online/story/0,3605,1433697,00.html.

Allen, M. (2009) 'Tim O'Reilly and Web 2.0: The economics of memetic liberty and control', *Communication, Politics & Culture*, 2 (2): 6–23.

Anderson, K., Nafus, D., Rattenbury, T. and Aipperspach, R. (2009) 'Numbers have qualities too: Experiences with ethno-mining', *Ethnographic Praxis in Industry Conference Proceedings*, (1): 123–40.

Anderson, L. (2011) 'Demystifying the Arab Spring', *Foreign Affairs*, May/June. Retrieved from www.ssrresourcecentre.org/wp-content/uploads/2011/06/Anderson-Demystifying-the-Arab-Spring.pdf.

Andrejevic, M. (2011) 'Social network exploitation', in Z. Paparcharissi (ed.), *A Networked Self*. New York: Routledge. pp. 82–101.

Bamman, D., O'Connor, B. and Smith, N. (2012) 'Censorship and deletion practices in Chinese social media', *First Monday*, 17 (3). Retrieved from www.uic.edu/htbin/cgiwrap/bin/ojs/index.php/fm/article/view/3943/3169.

Banks, J. and Humphreys, S. (2008) 'The labour of user co-creators', *Convergence*, 14 (4): 401–418.

Barlow, J. P. (1996) *A Cyberspace Independence Declaration*. Retrieved from http://w2.eff.org/Censorship/Internet_censorship_bills/barlow_0296.declaration.

Barthes, R. (1966 [1977]) 'The death of the author', in S. Heath (ed.), *Image – Music – Text*. New York: Hill and Wang. pp. 142–48.

Batchen, G. (2001). *Each Wild Idea: Writing, Photography, History*. Cambridge, MA: MIT Press.

Baym, N. (1998) 'The emergence of on-line community', in S. Jones (ed.), *CyberSociety 2.0: Revisiting Computer-mediated Communication and Community*. Thousand Oaks, CA: Sage. pp. 35–68.

BBC Editorial (2002) 'Amazon turns its first profit', *BBC News*, 22 January. Retrieved from http://news.bbc.co.uk/1/hi/business/1775294.stm.

Bell, D. and Kennedy, B. (2000) *The Cybercultures Reader*. London: Routledge.

Beniger, J. R. (1986) *The Control Revolution: Technological and Economic Origins of the Information Society*. Cambridge, MA: Harvard University Press.

Bennett, W. L. (2008) 'Changing citizenship in the digital age', in W. L. Bennett (ed.), *Civic Life Online: Learning How Digital Media Can Engage Youth*. Cambridge, MA: MIT Press. pp. 1–24.

Bennett, W. L., Wells, C. and Rank, A. (2009) 'Young citizens and civic learning: Two paradigms of citizenship in the digital age', *Citizenship Studies*, 13 (2): 105–120.

Berlant, L. (1998) 'Intimacy': A Special Issue. *Critical Inquiry*, 24 (2): 281–88.

Berners-Lee, T. (2006) Interviewed by Scott Laningham, *Developerworks*. Retrieved from www.ibm.com/developerworks/podcast/dwi/cm-int082206txt.html.

Bolter, J. and Grusin, R. (1999) *Remediation: Understanding New Media*. Cambridge, MA: MIT Press.

Bourdieu, P. (1984 [1979]) *Distinction: A Social Critique of the Judgment of Taste*, trans. R. Nice. Cambridge, MA: Harvard University Press.

Bourriaud, N. (2002) *Relational Aesthetics*, trans. S. Pleasance and F. Woods. Dijon: Les Presses du Réel.

boyd, d. (2004) *Revenge of the User: Lessons from Creator/User Battles*. Paper presented at the O'Reilly Emerging Technology Conference, February. Retrieved from www.danah.org/papers/talks/Etech2004.html.

boyd, d. (2008) 'Facebook's privacy trainwreck: Exposure, invasion, and social convergence', *Convergence: The International Journal of Research into New Media Technologies*, 14 (1): 13–20.

boyd, d. (2009) 'How can qualitative internet researchers define the boundaries of their projects? A response to Christine Hine', in A. N. Markham and N. K. Baym (eds), *Internet Inquiry: Conversations About Method*. Thousand Oaks, CA: Sage. pp. 26–32.

boyd, d. (2011) 'Social network sites as networked publics: Affordances, dynamics, and implications', in Z. Papacharissi (ed.), *A Networked Self: Identity, Community and Culture on Social Network Sites*. New York: Routledge. pp. 39–58.

boyd, d. and Crawford, K. (2011) *Six Provocations for Big Data*. Retrieved from http://papers.ssrn.com/sol3/papers.cfm?abstract_id=1926431.

boyd, d. and Crawford, K. (2012) 'Critical questions for big data', *Information, Communication & Society*, 15 (5): 662–79.

boyd, d. and Ellison, N. B. (2007) 'Social network sites: Definition, history, and scholarship', *Journal of Computer Mediated Communication*, 13 (1). Retrieved from http://jcmc.indiana.edu/vol13/issue1/boyd.ellison.html.

boyd, d. and Hargittai, E. (2010) 'Facebook privacy settings: Who cares?', *First Monday* (15) 8. Retrieved from http://firstmonday.org/htbin/cgiwrap/bin/ojs/index.php/fm/article/view/3086/2589.

boyd, d. and Marwick, A. E. (2011) *Social Privacy in Networked Publics: Teens' Attitudes, Practices, and Strategies*. Retrieved from http://papers.ssrn.com/sol3/papers.cfm?abstract_id=1925128.

Boyd, J. (2005) 'The only gadget you'll ever need', *New Scientist*, 5 Mar: 28.

Broun, E. (2007) 'Keynote address: Envisioning American Art 2.0', *First Monday* (12) 7. Retrieved from http://firstmonday.org/htbin/cgiwrap/bin/ojs/index.php/fm/article/view/1919/1801.

Bruns, A. (2005) 'Some exploratory notes on produsers and produsage'. *Snurblog*, 3 November. Retrieved from http://snurb.info/index.php?q=node/329.

Bruns, A. (2008) *Blogs, Wikipedia, Second Life, and Beyond: From Production to Produsage*. New York: Peter Lang.

Bruns, A. and Jacobs, J. (2006) *Uses of Blogs*. New York: Peter Lang.

Bruns, A., Wilson, J. A. and Saunders, B. J. (2008) 'Building spaces for hyperlocal citizen journalism', in *Proceedings Association of Internet Researchers 2008: Internet Research 9.0: Rethinking Community, Rethinking Place*. Copenhagen, Denmark.

Bruns, A., Wilson, J. A. and Saunders, B. J. (2009) 'Citizen journalism as social networking: Reporting the 2007 Australian Federal Election', in S. Allan and E. Thorsen (eds), *Citizen Journalism: Global Perspectives*. New York: Peter Lang. pp. 197–208.

Bruns, A., Burgess, J., Crawford, K. and Shaw, F. (2012) *#qldfloods and @ QPSMedia: Crisis Communication on Twitter in the 2011 South East Queensland Floods*. Brisbane: ARC Centre of Excellence for Creative Industries and Innovation.

Burgess, J. E. (2007) 'Vernacular creativity and new media'. PhD thesis, Queensland University of Technology. Retrieved from http://eprints.qut.edu.au/16378/.

Burgess, J. E. (2008) '"All your chocolate rain are belong to us?" Viral video, YouTube and the dynamics of participatory culture', in G. Lovink and S. Niedere (eds), *The Video Vortex*. Amsterdam: Institute of Network Cultures. pp. 101–111.

Burgess, J. E., Foth, M. and Klaebe, H. G. (2006) 'Everyday creativity as civic engagement: A cultural citizenship view of new media', *Communications Policy & Research Forum*. Sydney, Australia. Retrieved from http://eprints.qut.edu.au/5056/1/5056_1.pdf.

Burkholder, L. (ed.) (1992) *Philosophy and the Computer*. Oxford: Westview Press.

Butler, P. (2010) *Visualizing Friendships*, 13 December. Retrieved from www.facebook.com/note.php?note_id=469716398919.

Castells, M. (1996) *The Rise of the Network Society: The Information Age: Economy, Society and Culture, Vol. I*. Cambridge, MA: Oxford University Press.

Castells, M. (2001) *The Internet Galaxy: Reflections on the Internet, Business and Society*. Oxford: Oxford University Press.

Cheng, Y. (2010) 'Millions fall in love with SNS games', *China Daily*, 12 February. Retrieved from www.chinadaily.com.cn/china/2010–02/12/content_9466051.htm.

Chesher, C. (2012) 'Between image and information: The iPhone camera in the history of photography', in L. Hjorth, J. Burgess, and I. Richardson (eds), *Studying Mobile Media: Cultural Technologies, Mobile Communication, and the iPhone*. London/New York: Routledge. pp. 98–117.

Chun, W. (2006) *Control and Freedom*. Cambridge, MA: MIT Press.

Cincotta, K., Ashford, K. and Michael, K. (2011) 'The new privacy predators', *Women's Health*. Retrieved from www.purehacking.com/sites/default/files/uploads/2011_11_00_Australian_Womens_Health_November.pdf.

CIW (China Internet Watch) (2012) *CIW China Internet Insights* (CCII). Retrieved from www.chinainternetwatch.com/whitepaper/china-internet-statistics/.

Clarke, R. (1999) *The Willingness of Net-Consumers to Pay: A Lack-of-Progress Report*. Retrieved from www.rogerclarke.com/EC/WillPay.html.

Clarke, R. (2000) 'Information Wants to be Free ...', 24 February. Retrieved from www.rogerclarke.com/II/IWtbF.html.

Cleaver, H. M., Jr. (1998) 'The Zapatista effect: The Internet and the rise of an alternative political fabric', *Journal of International Affairs*, 51 (2): 621–40.

Clifford, J. and Marcus, G. E. (eds) (1986) *Writing Culture: The Poetics and Politics of Ethnography*. Berkeley, CA: University of California Press.

CNNIC (China Internet Network Information Center) (2009) *Statistical Survey Report on the Internet Development in China*. Retrieved from www.cnnic.cn/uploadfiles/pdf/2009/3/23/131303.pdf.

CNNIC (2011) *Statistical Survey Report on Internet Development in China.* Retrieved from http://www1.cnnic.cn/IDR/ReportDownloads/201209/P020120 904421102801754.pdf.

CNNIC (2012) Chinese Internet Network Information Center: 'The 30th Survey Report', http://www1.cnnic.cn/IDR/ReportDownloads/201209/t20120928_36586.htm.

Coleman, J. S. (1988) 'Social capital in the creation of human capital', *American Journal of Sociology*, 94: 95–120.

Collins, J. (1996) '"High Stakes winners": Netscape's Marc Andreessen', *Time Magazine*, 19 February ("The Golden Geeks" issue). Retrieved from www.time.com/time/magazine/article/0,9171,984131,00.html.

Corneliussen, H. and Rettberg, J. W. (2008) *Digital Culture, Play, and Identity: A World of Warcraft Reader*. Cambridge, MA: MIT Press.

Crawford, K. (2009) 'Following you: Disciplines of listening in social media', *Continuum*, 23 (4): 523–35.

Crawford, K. (2010) 'Listening, not lurking: The neglected form of participation', in H. Grief, L. Hjorth and A. Lasén (eds), *Cultures of Participation*. Berlin: Peter Lang.

Cresswell, T. (2009) *Place*. Retrieved from www.elsevierdirect.com/brochures/hugy/SampleContent/Place.pdf.

Curtis, P. (1996) 'Mudding: Social phenomena in text-based virtual communities', in P. Ludlow (ed.), *High Noon on the Electronic Frontier: Conceptual Issues in Cyberspace*. Cambridge, MA: MIT Press.

Dahlgren, L. (2001) 'The Internet and democratic discourse: Exploring the prospects of online deliberative forums extending the public sphere', *Information, Communication & Society*, (4): 615–33.

de Certeau, M. (1984) *The Practice of Everyday Life*, trans. S. Rendall. Berkeley, CA: The University of California Press.

de Souza e Silva, A. and Hjorth, L. (2009) 'Playful urban spaces: A historical approach to mobile games', *Simulation and Gaming*, 40 (5): 602–625.

de Souza e Silva, A. and Sutko, D. M. (2009) *Digital Cityscapes: Merging Digital and Urban Playspaces*. New York: Peter Lang.

de Souza e Silva, A. and Frith, J. (2012) *Mobile Interfaces in Public Spaces: Locational Privacy, Control, and Urban Sociability*. New York: Routledge.

Diamond, L. and Plattner, M. (eds) (2012) *Liberation Technology: Social Media and the Struggle for Democracy*. Baltimore, MD: Johns Hopkins University.

DiNucci, D. (1999) 'Fragmented future', *Print*, 53 (4): 32. Retrieved from www.cdinucci.com/darcy2/articles/print/printarticle7.html.

Du Gay, P., Hall, S., Janes, L., Mackay, H. and Negus, K.(1997). *Doing Cultural Studies: The story of the Sony Walkman*. Thousand Oaks, CA: Sage.

Ellison, N., Lane, C., Steinfeld, C. and Vitak, J. (2011) 'With a little help from my friends: How social network sites affect social capital processes', in Paparcharissi, Z. (ed.), *A Networked Self*. New York: Routledge. pp. 146–68.

Elmer-Dewitt, P. (1993) 'First nation in cyberspace', *TIME International*, 6 December, No. 49.

Falkheimer, J. and Jansson, A. (eds) (2006) *Geographies of Communication: The Spatial Turn in Media Studies*. Götenberg: Nordicom.

Farman, J. (2011) *Mobile Interface Theory*. London: Routledge.

Fei, C. (2011) Personal interview with L. Hjorth, September.

Fleming, D. (2005) *Managing Change in Museums*. Keynote presented at the Museum and Change International Conference, 8–10 November, National Museum, Prague.

Flew, T. and Wilson, J. A. (2010) 'Journalism as social networking: The Australian youdecide project and the 2007 federal election', *Journalism: Theory, Practice and Criticism*, 11 (2): 131–47.

Fortunati, L. (2002) 'Italy: Stereotypes, true and false', in J. E. Katz and M. Aakhus (eds), *Perpetual Contact: Mobile Communications, Private Talk, Public Performance*. Cambridge: Cambridge University Press. pp. 42–62.

Foster, H. (1996) *The Return of the Real: The Avant-Garde at the End of the Century*. Cambridge, MA: MIT Press.

Fujimoto, K. (2005) 'The third-stage paradigm: Territory machine from the girls' pager revolution to mobile aesthetics', in M. Ito, D. Okabe and M. Matsuda (eds), *Personal, Portable, Pedestrian: Mobile Phones In Japanese Life*. Cambridge, MA: MIT Press. pp. 77–102.

Garrett, K. R. (2006) 'Protest in an information society: A review of literature on social movements and new ICTs', Special Issue, *Information, Communication & Society*, 9 (2).

Gazzard, A. (2011) 'Location, location, location: Collecting space and place in mobile media', *Convergence*, 17 (4): 405–417.

German, K. (n.d.) 'Top 10 dot-com flops', *CNet.com*. Retrieved from www.cnet.com/1990–11136_1–6278387–1.html.

Geron, T. (2012) 'Facebook's $5 billion IPO filing: $3.7 billion in 2011 revenue', *Forbes*, 1 February. Retrieved from www.forbes.com/sites/tomiogeron/2012/02/01/facebooks-5-billion-ipo-filing-3–7-billion-in-2011-revenue/.

Gillespie, T. (2010) 'The politics of "platforms"', *New Media & Society*, 12 (3): 347–64.

Gillmor, D. (2006) *We the Media*. Sebastopol, CA: O'Reilly.

Goffman, E. (1959 [1990]) *The Presentation of Self in Everyday Life*. London: Penguin.

Goggin, G. (2011) *Global Mobile Media*. London: Routledge.

Goggin, G. and Hjorth, L. (2009) 'Waiting to participate: An introduction', *Communication, Culture & Politics*, 42 (2): 1–5.

Goggin, G. and McLelland, M. (eds) (2009) *Internationalizing Internet Studies*. London: Routledge.

Gordon, E. and de Souza e Silva, A. (2011) *Net Locality*. Chichester: Wiley.

Graham, P. (2006) *Interview About Web 2.0*. Retrieved from http://paulgraham.com/web20interview.html.

Gregg, M. (2011) *Work's Intimacy*. Cambridge: Polity.

Gross, R. and Acquisti, A. (2005) 'Information revelation and privacy in online social networks', *Proceedings of the 2005 ACM Workshop on Privacy in the Electronic Society, WPES 2005*. New York: ACM. pp. 71–80.

Habermas, J. (1989) *The Structural Transformation of the Public Sphere: An Inquiry into a Category of Bourgeois Society*. Cambridge, MA: MIT Press.

Haddon, L. (1999) 'The development of interactive games', in H. Mackay and T. O'Sullivan (eds), *The Media Reader: Continuity and Transformation*. London: Sage. pp. 305–327.

Hagel, J. (1997) *Net Gain: Expanding Markets Through Virtual Communities*. Boston, MA: Harvard Business Review Press.

Hall, S. (1973) *Encoding and Decoding in the Television Discourse*. Birmingham: Centre for Cultural Studies, University of Birmingham.

Hampton, K. N., Sessions Goulet, L., Rainie, L. and Purcell, K. (2011) *Social Networking Sites and Our Lives*. 16 June. Retrieved from http://pewinternet.org/~/media//Files/Reports/2011/PIP%20-%20Social%20networking%20sites%20and%20our%20lives.pdf.

Haythornthwaite, C. and Wellman, B. (1998) 'Work, friendship, and media use for information exchange in a networked organization', *Journal of the American Society for Information Science*, 49 (12): 1101–1114.

Herzfeld, M. (1997) *Cultural Intimacy: Social Poetics in the Nation State*. New York: Routledge.

Hine, C. (1998) *Virtual Ethnography*. Paper From Internet Research And Information For Social Scientists Conference, 25–27 March, University Of Bristol, UK.

Hinton, S. and Whitelaw, M. (2010) *Exploring the Digital Commons: An Approach to the Visualization of Large Heritage Datasets*. Paper presented at Electronic Visualisation and the Arts Conference, 5–7 July, London.

Hjorth, L. (2003) Kawaii@keitai', in N. Gottlieb and M. McLelland (eds), *Japanese Cybercultures*. New York: Routledge. pp. 50–59.

Hjorth, L. (2005) 'Locating mobility: Practices of co-presence and the persistence of the postal metaphor in SMS/MMS mobile phone customization in Melbourne', *Fibreculture Journal*, (6). Retrieved from http://journal.fibreculture.org/issue6/issue6_hjorth.html.

Hjorth, L. (2007) 'Snapshots of almost contact: A case study on South Korea', Special Issue, G. Goggin (ed.), *Continuum*, 21 (2): 227–38.

Hjorth, L. (2012) 'iPersonal: A case study of the politics of the personal', in L. Hjorth, J. Burgess and I. Richardson (eds), *Studying Mobile Media: Cultural Technologies, Mobile Communication, and the iPhone*. New York: Routledge. pp. 190–212.

Hjorth, L. and Arnold M. (2012) 'Home and away: A case study of students and social media in Shanghai', in P. Law (ed.), *New Connectivities in China: Virtual, Actual and Local Interactions*. Dordrecht: Springer. pp. 171–83.

Hjorth, L. and Arnold, M. (2013) *Online@AsiaPacific: Creativity, Literacy and Politics in the Asia–Pacific Region*. London: Asia's Transformation series, Routledge.

Hjorth, L. and Chan, D. (2009) *Gaming Cultures and Place in Asia-Pacific*. New York: Routledge.

Hjorth, L. and Gu, K. (2012) 'Placing, emplacing and embodied visualities: A case study of smartphone visuality and location-based social media in Shanghai, China', *Continuum*, 26 (5): 699–713.

Hjorth, L. and Kim, H. (2005) 'Being there and being here: Gendered customising of mobile 3G practices through a case study in Seoul', *Convergence*, 11: 49–55.

Hjorth, L. and Kim, Y. (2011) 'The mourning after: A commentary on crisis management in Japan post 3.11', *Television & New Media Journal*, 12 (6): 552–59.

Hjorth, L. Burgess J. and Richardson I. (eds) (2012) *Studying Mobile Media: Cultural Technologies, Mobile Communication, and the iPhone*. New York: Routledge.

Hjorth, L., Wilken, R. and Gu, K. (2012) 'Ambient intimacy: A case study of the iPhone, presence, and location-based social networking in Shanghai, China', in L. Hjorth, J. Burgess and I. Richardson (eds), *Studying Mobile Media: Cultural*

Technologies, Mobile Communication, and the iPhone. London: Routledge. pp. 43–62.

Holley, R. (2009) *Many Hands Make Light Work: Public Collaborative OCR Text Correction in Australian Historic Newspapers*. Retrieved from www.nla.gov.au/openpublish/index.php/nlasp/article/view/1406/1688.

Horkheimer, M. and Adorno, T. (2002[1944]) 'The Culture Industry': Dialectic of *Enlightenment*. Stanford, CA: Stanford University Press.

Hou, J. (2011) 'Uses and gratifications of social games: Blending social networking and game play', *First Monday*, 16 (7). Retrieved from http://firstmonday.org/htbin/cgiwrap/bin/ojs/index.php/fm/article/view/3517/3020.

Howard, P., Duffy, A., Freelon, D., Hussain, M., Mari, W. and Mazaid, M. (2011) 'Opening closed regimes: What was the role of social media during the Arab Spring?', *Project on Information Technology and Political Islam*, Research Memo 2011.1. Seattle, WA: University of Washington.

Huhtamo, E. (2002) *Virtual Museums and Public Understanding of Science and Culture*. Paper presented at Nobel Symposium (NS 120), Stockholm, Sweden.

Huizinga, J. (1938 [1970]) *Homo Ludens: A Study of the Play Element in Culture*. London: Temple Smith.

Ingold, T (2008) 'Bindings against boundaries: entanglements of life in an open world', *Environment and Planning A*, 40: 1796–1810.

ISG (Information Solutions Group) (2010) *2010 Social Gaming Research*. Retrieved from www.infosolutionsgroup.com/2011_PopCap_Mobile_Phone_Games_Presentation.pdf.

Ito, M. (2002) 'Mobiles and the appropriation of place', *Receiver*, 8. Retrieved from http://academic.evergreen.edu/curricular/evs/readings/itoShort.pdf.

Ito, M. (2005) 'Introduction: Personal, portable, pedestrian', in M. Ito, D. Okabe and M. Matsuda (eds), *Personal, Portable, Pedestrian: Mobile Phones in Japanese Life*. Cambridge, MA: MIT Press. pp. 1–16.

Ito, M. and Okabe, D. (2005) *Intimate Visual Co-Presence*. Paper presented at Ubicomp, 11–14 September, Tokyo, Japan. Retrieved from www.itofisher.com/mito/.

Ito, M. and Okabe, D. (2006) 'Everyday contexts of camera phone use: Steps towards technosocial ethnographic frameworks', in J. Höflich and M. Hartmann (eds), *Mobile Communication In Everyday Life: An Ethnographic View*. Berlin: Frank & Timme. pp. 79–102.

Ito, M., boyd, d. and Horst, H. (2008) *Digital Youth Research*. Retrieved from http://digitalyouth.ischool.berkeley.edu/.

ITU (International Telecommunications Union) (2011) *Measuring the Information Society*. Retrieved from www.itu.int/ITU-D/ict/publications/idi/material/2011/MIS_2011_without_annex_5.pdf.

Jenkins, H. (1992) *Fans, Bloggers, and Gamers: Essays on Participatory Culture*. New York: New York University Press.

Jenkins, H. (2006) *Convergence Culture: Where Old and New Media Intersect*. New York: New York University Press.

Jones, M. (2009) *Data as Seductive Material*, 19 February. Retrieved from www.slideshare.net/blackbeltjones/data-as-seductive-material-spring-summit-ume-march09.

Juul, J. (2009) *A Casual Revolution: Reinventing Video Games and their Players*. Cambridge, MA: MIT Press.

Kamvar, S. and Harris, J. (2009) *We Feel Fine: An Almanac of Human Emotion*. New York: Scribner.

Kember, S. (1998) *Virtual Anxiety: Photography, New Technologies and Subjectivity*. Manchester: Manchester University Press.

Kendall, L. (2002) *Hanging Out in the Virtual Pub*. Berkeley, CA: University of California Press.

Kirman, B. (2010) 'Emergence and playfulness in social games', in *Proceedings of the 14th International Academic MindTrek Conference: Envisioning Future Media Environments*. New York: ACM. pp. 71–7.

Kirman, B., Lawson, S. and Linehan, C. (2009) *Gaming On and Off the Social Graph: The Social Structure of Facebook Games*. IEEE International Conference on Social Computing (SocialCom'09); Symposium on Social Computing Applications, 4: 627–32.

Klose, A. (2011) Personal interview with L. Hjorth, September.

Kogo, T. (2011) Personal interview with L. Hjorth, September.

Koskela, H. (2004) 'Webcams, TV shows and mobile phones: Empowering exhibitionism', *Surveillance and Society*, 2 (2/3): 199–215.

Kücklich, J. (2005) 'Precarious playbour: Modders and the digital games industry', *Fibreculture Journal*, 5. Retrieved from http://journal.fibreculture.org/issue5/kucklich.html.

Leadbeater, C., Miller, P. and Demos (2004) *The Pro-Am Revolution: How Enthusiasts are Changing Our Society and Economy*. London: Demos.

Lee, D.-H. (2005) 'Women's creation of camera phone culture', *Fibreculture Journal*, 6. Retrieved from www.fibreculture.org/journal/issue6/issue6_donghoo_print.html.

Lee, D.-H. (2009) 'Mobile snapshots and private/public boundaries', *Knowledge, Technology & Policy*, 22 (3): 161–71.

Levine, R. et al. (2000) *The Cluetrain Manifesto: The End of Business as Usual*. Cambridge, MA: Perseus.

Lewis, M. (2000) *The New New Thing: A Silicon Valley Story*. New York: Penguin.

Licoppe, C. (2004) '"Connected" presence: The emergence of a new repertoire for managing social relationships in a changing communication technoscape' *Environment and Planning Design: Society and Space*, 22 (1): 135–156.

Licoppe, C. and Inada, Y. (2006) 'Emergent uses of a location aware multiplayer game: The interactional consequences of mediated encounters', *Mobilities*, 1 (1): 39–61.

Livingstone, S. (2005) *Critical Debates in Internet Studies: Reflections on an Emerging Field*. London: LSE Research Online. Retrieved from http://eprints.lse.ac.uk/1011.

Lovink, G. (2012) *Networks Without a Cause: A Critique of Social Media*. Cambridge, UK: Polity Press.

Luke, R. (2006) 'The phoneur: Mobile commerce and the digital pedagogies of the wireless Web', in P. Trifonas (ed.), *Communities of Difference: Culture, Language, Technology*. London: Palgrave. pp. 185–204.

Madianou, M. and Miller, D. (2012) *Migration and New Media: Transnational Families and Polymedia*. New York: Routledge.

Malaby, T. M. (2007) 'Beyond play: A new approach to games', *Games and Culture*, 2 (2): 95–113.

Marcus, G. E. and Myers, F. R. (1995) 'The traffic in art and culture', in G. E. Marcus and F. R. Myers (eds), *Traffic in Culture*. Berkley, CA: University of California Press. pp. 1–54.

Marwick, A. (2008) 'To catch a predator? The MySpace moral panic', *First Monday*, 13 (6). Retrieved from http://firstmonday.org/htbin/cgiwrap/bin/ojs/index.php/fm/article/view/2152.

Massey, D. (2005) *For Space*. London: Sage.

McVeigh, B. (2000) 'How Hello Kitty commodifies the cute, cool and camp: "Consumutopia" versus "control" in Japan', *Journal Of Material Culture*, 5 (2): 291–312.

Meikle, G. and Redden, G. (2010) *News Online: Transformations and Continuities*. London: Palgrave.

Michael, M. G. and Michael, K. (2010) 'Towards a state of überveillence', *IEEE Technology and Society Magazine*, 29 (2): 9–16.

Miller, D. (2011) *Tales from Facebook*. Cambridge: Polity.

Miller, D. and Slater, D. (2001) *The Internet: An Ethnographic Approach*. London: Berg.

Milne, E. (2004) 'Magic bits of paste-board', *M/C: A Journal of Media and Culture*, 7. Retrieved from www.media-culture.org.au/0401/02-milne.php.

Mørk Petersen, S. (2008) 'Common banality: The affective character of photo sharing, everyday life and produsage cultures'. Doctoral dissertation, IT University of Copenhagen.

Munster, A. and Murphie, A. (2009) 'Web 2.0 is a doing word', *Fibreculture Journal*, 14. Retrieved from http://fourteen.fibreculturejournal.org/.

Nakamura, L. (2002) *Cybertypes: Race, Ethnicity, and Identity on the Internet*. New York: Routledge.

Nardi, B. A. (2010) *My Life as a Night Elf Priest: An Anthropological Account of World of Warcraft*. Ann Arbor, MI: University of Michigan Press.

National Endowment for the Arts (2010) *Audience 2.0: How Technology Influences Arts Participation*, June. Retrieved from www.nea.gov/research/new-media-report/index.html.

Nugroho, Y. and Syarief, S. S. (2012) *Beyond Click-Activism? New Media and Political Processes in Contemporary Indonesia*. Jakarta: Friedrich-Ebert-Stiftung, fesmedia Asia series. Retrieved from www.fes.de/cgi-bin/gbv.cgi?id=09240&ty=pdf.

Okabe, D. and Ito, M. (2003) 'Camera phones changing the definition of picture-worthy', *Japan Media Review*, 28 August. Retrieved from www.ojr.org/japan/wireless/1062208524.php.

Okada, T. (2005) 'Youth culture and the shaping of Japanese mobile media: Personalization and the Keitai Internet as Multimedia', in M. Ito, D. Okabe and M. Matsuda (eds), *Personal, Portable, Pedestrian: Mobile Phones in Japanese Life*. Cambridge, MA: MIT Press. pp. 41–60.

Oldenburg, R. (1989) *The Great Good Place: Cafes, Coffee Shops, Community Centers, Beauty Parlors, General Stores, Bars, Hangouts, and How They Get You Through the Day*. New York: Paragon.

O'Reilly, T. (2005) *What is Web 2.0: Design Patterns and Business Models for the Next Generation of Software*. Retrieved from http://oreilly.com/web2/archive/what-is-web-20.html.

Palmer, D. (2012) 'iPhone photography: Mediating visions of social space', in L. Hjorth, J. Burgess and I. Richardson (eds), *Studying Mobile Media: Cultural Technologies, Mobile Communication, and the iPhone*. New York: Routledge. pp. 85–97.

Parks, M. R. (2011) 'Social network sites as virtual communities', in Z. Papacharissi (ed.), *A Networked Self: Identity, Community and Culture on Social Network Sites*. New York: Routledge. pp. 105–123.

Pearce, C. (with Artemesia) (2009) *Communities of Play: Emergent Cultures in Multiplayer Games and Virtual Worlds*. Cambridge, MA: MIT Press.

Perkel, D. (2012) 'Making art, creating infrastructure: deviantART and the production of the web'. Doctoral dissertation, University of California. Retrieved from http://people.ischool.berkeley.edu/~dperkel/diss/DanPerkel-dissertation-2011_update.pdf.

Pickerill, J. (2010) *Cyberprotest: Environmental Activism Online*. Manchester: Manchester University Press.

Pink, S. (2009) *Doing Sensory Ethnography*. London: Sage.

Pink, S. (2011) 'Sensory digital photography: Re-thinking "moving" and the image', *Visual Studies*, 26 (1): 4–13.

Playfish (2012) *Electronic Arts Acquires Playfish*. Retrieved from www.playfish.com/press_releases/?release=09_11_2009.

Putnam, R. (2000) *Bowling Alone*. New York: Simon and Schuster.

Qiu, J. L. (2008) 'Wireless working-class ICTs and the Chinese informational city', *The Journal of Urban Technology*, 15 (3): 57–77.

Rao, V. (2008) 'Facebook applications and playful mood: The construction of Facebook as a "third place"', in *Proceedings of the 14th International Academic MindTrek Conference: Envisioning Future Media Environments* (MindTrek '10). New York: ACM. pp. 8–12.

Reid, E. (1995) 'Virtual worlds: Culture and imagination', in S. Jones (ed.), *CyberSociety: Computer-Mediated Communication and Community*. Thousand Oaks, CA: Sage.

Rheingold, H. (1993) *The Virtual Community: Homesteading on the Electronic Frontier*. Reading, MA: Addison-Wesley.

Rheingold, H. (2002) *Smart Mobs: The Next Social Revolution*. Cambridge, MA: Perseus.

Rheingold, H. (2008) 'Using participatory media and public voice to encourage civic engagement', in W. L. Bennett (ed.), *Civic Life Online: Learning How Digital Media Can Engage Youth*. Cambridge, MA: MIT Press. pp. 97–118.

Richardson, I. (2011) 'The hybrid ontology of mobile gaming', *Convergence*, 17 (4): 419–30.

Richardson, I. and Wilken, R. (2012) 'Parerga of the third screen: Mobile media, place, and presence', in R. Wilken and G. Goggin (eds), *Mobile Technology and Place*. New York: Routledge. pp. 198–212.

Rossi, L. (2009) *Playing Your Network: Gaming in Social Network Sites*. Breaking New Ground: Innovation in Games, Play, Practice and Theory. Proceedings of Digital Games Research Association Conference 2009. Retrieved from www.digra.org/dl/db/09287.20599.pdf.

Rubinstein, D. and Sluis, K. (2008) 'A life more photographic: Mapping the networked image', *Photographies*, 1 (1): 9–28.

Rushkoff, D. (1994) *Cyberia: Life in the Trenches of Cyberspace*. New York: Clinamen Press.

Salah, A. A. (2010) *The Online Potential of Art Creation and Dissemination: deviantART as the Next Art Venue*. Paper presented at Electronic Visualisation and the Arts Conference, 5–7 July, London.

Salen, K. and Zimmerman, E. (2003) *Rules of Play: Game Design Fundamentals*. Cambridge, MA: MIT Press.

SEO Sydney Blog (2009) *Facebook Australia: User Statistics & Demographics*. www. seosydneyblog.com/2009/08/facebook-australia-user-statistics.html.

Shin, D.-H. and Shin, Y.-J. (2011) 'Why do people play social network games?', *Computers in Human Behavior*, 27: 852–61.

Shirky, C. (2008) *Here Comes Everybody*. The Aspen Ideas Festival, 30 June–8 July, Aspen Colorado. Retrieved from www.channels.com/episodes/show/12772338/ Clay-Shirky-Here-Comes-Everybody?page=5.

Shirky, C. (2009) *Here Comes Everybody: The Power of Organizing Without Organizations*. New York: Penguin.

Simon, N. (2012) *Museum 2.0*. Retrieved from http://museumtwo.blogspot.com.au/.

Sonnenfeld, B. (Director) (1997) *Men in Black* [Film]. United States: Amblin Entertainment.

Soukup, C. (2006) 'Computer-mediated communication as a virtual third place: Building Oldenburg's great good places on the World Wide Web', *New Media & Society*, 8 (3): 421–40.

Stallabrass, J. (2010) 'Can art history digest net art?', in D. Daniels and G. Reisinger (eds), *Net Pioneers 1.0: Contextualizing Early Net-based Art*. New York: Sternberg.

Standage, T. (1998) *The Victorian Internet: The Remarkable Story of the Telegraph and the Nineteenth Century's On-line Pioneers*. London: Weidenfeld & Nicolson.

Steinkuehler, C. and Williams, D. (2006) 'Where everybody knows your (screen) name: Online games as "third places"', *Journal of Computer-Mediated Communication*, 11 (4). Retrieved from http://jcmc.indiana.edu/vol11/issue4/steinkuehler.html.

Stephenson, N. (1992) *Snow Crash*. London: Penguin.

Stuart, A. (2007) 'Citizen journalism and the rise of "mass self-communication": Reporting the London bombings', *Global Media Journal*, 1 (1). Retrieved from www.commarts.uws.edu.au/gmjau/iss1_2007/pdf/HC_FINAL_Stuart%20 Allan.pdf.

Surowiecki, J. (2004) *The Wisdom of Crowds: Why the Many Are Smarter Than the Few and How Collective Wisdom Shapes Business, Economies, Societies, and Nations*. New York: Doubleday.

Taylor, T. L. (2006) *Play Between Worlds Exploring Online Game Culture*. Cambridge, MA: MIT Press.

Thelwall, M. (2008) 'Social networks, gender, and friending: An analysis of MySpace member profiles', *Journal of American Social Information Sciences*, 59: 1321–30.

Thorp, J. (2009) 'Just landed: Processing, Twitter, MetaCarta and hidden data', *blprnt.blg*. 11 May. Retrieved from http://blog.blprnt.com/blog/blprnt/just-landed-processing-twitter-metacarta-hidden-data.

Trant, J. (2006) 'Exploring the potential for social tagging and folksonomy in art museums: Proof of concept', *New Review of Hypermedia and Multimedia*, 12 (1): 83–105.

Turkle, S. (1984) *The Second Self: Computers and the Human Spirit*. New York: Simon and Schuster.

Turkle, S. (1995) *Life on the Screen: Identity in the Age of the Internet*. New York: Simon and Schuster.

Turkle, S. (2011) *Alone Together: Why We Expect More from Technology and Less from Each Other*. New York: Basic Books.

Turner, B. (2005) 'Information-age guerrillas: The communication strategies of the Zapatistas', *M/C Journal*, 8 (2). Retrieved from http://journal.media-culture.org.au/0506/01-turner.php.

Vaidhyanathan, S. (2011) *The Googlization of Everything*. Berkeley, CA: University of California Press.

Villi, M. (2013) 'Visual mobile communication on the internet: Publishing and messaging camera phone photograph patterns', in Cumiskey, K. and Hjorth, L. (eds), *Seamlessly Mobile: Mobile Media practices, presence & politics*. New York: Routledge.

Wacjman, J., Bittman, M. and Brown, J. (2009) 'The mobile phone, perpetual contact and time pressure', *Work, Employment and Society*, 23 (4): 673–91.

Warner, M. (2002) *Publics and Counterpublics*. Cambridge, MA: MIT Press.

Weiser, M. (1991) 'The computer for the 21st century', *Scientific American*, 265 (3): 94–104.

Wellman, B. (2003) 'The social affordances of the Internet for networked individualism', *Journal of Computer-Mediated Communication*, 8 (3). Retrieved from http://jcmc.indiana.edu/vol8/issue3/wellman.html.

Wellman, B. and Gulia, M. (1999) 'Net surfers don't ride alone: Virtual communities as communities', in P. Kollock and M. A. Smith (eds), *Communities in Cyberspace*. London: Routledge.

Wellman, B. and Haythornthwaite, C. A. (eds) (2002) *The Internet in Everyday Life*. Oxford: Blackwell.

Wilken, R. and Goggin, G. (2012) *Mobile Technology and Place*. London: Routledge.

Williams, D., Ducheneaut, N., Xiong, L., Zhang, Y., Yee, N. and Nickell, E. (2006) 'From tree house to barracks: The social life of guilds in World of Warcraft', *Games and Culture*, 1 (4): 338–61.

Wilson, J. (2011) 'Playing with politics: Political fans and Twitter faking in post-broadcast democracy', *Convergence*, 17 (4): 445–61.

Xiao, A. (2010) 'Always social: Social media art (2004–2008), Part One', *Hyperallergic*. Retrieved from http://hyperallergic.com/6644/social-media-art-pt-1/.

Yang, K. C., Ho, K. C., Kluver, R. and Yang, C. C. (2003) *Asia@com*. London: Routledge.

Yee, N. (2006) 'The demographics, motivations and derived experiences of users of massively-multiuser online graphical environments', *PRESENCE: Teleoperators and Virtual Environments*, 15: 309–329.

Zuckerman, E. (2008) *Cute Cat Theory of Digital Activism*. Paper presented at the O'Reilly ETech Conference, 3–6 March. Retrieved from http://en.oreilly.com/et2008/public/schedule/detail/1597.

Zynga (2012) *Zynga Reports Second Quarter 2012 Financial Results*. Retrieved from http://investor.zynga.com/releasedetail.cfm?ReleaseID=695419.

Index